"The amazing human spirit is shared in every page of this book. The stories will inspire you with your own ability to transform your life. Read it twice - once with your mind and once with your heart."

— PATRICIA J. CRANE, PH.D. Heart Inspired Presentations, LLC. Author of *Ordering from the Cosmic Kitchen: The Essential Guide to Powerful, Nourishing Affirmations.* www.drpatriciacrane.com

"Never before in the history of women is our personal and collective power potential so evident; ***Empowering Transformations for Women*** vibrantly shares stories of both that power potential and the reclamation of it. Our virtual sisterhood becomes a moving and tangible reality when seen through these poignant stories of insightful triumph, 'a-ha moments' and reclamation of sovereignty at the highest levels. This book is a must-read for anyone—woman or man—who seeks greater awareness and understanding inspired by these heroines who live amongst us."

— LYNN SCHEURELL. Creative Catalyst. www.MyCreativeCatalyst.com

"Women have supported, inspired and encouraged one another since time immemorial. How moved I was to hear the authentic voices of triumph echo within these powerful stories. It was a symphony. It was a privilege."

— MARY JANE HURLEY BRANT, M.S., CGP. Psychotherapist and Author of *When Every Day Matters* (Simple Abundance Press). www.WhenEveryDayMatters.com

"Over my years as a personal growth teacher I have found that the one thing that brings about "change" in one's life is inspiration. Inspiration is the lifeblood of transformation. Reading these beautiful stories will re-awaken the inner flame in your heart and bring you back to connection with your true self. This book is a gift beyond words!"

— SKIP LACKEY - President of The Journey and Conscious Company - North America. www.thejourneyusa.com

"If you want to be moved, inspired, and uplifted, give yourself the gift of *Empowering Transformations for Women*. I was in awe at the courage and resiliency of these brave women who faced insurmountable challenges with grace and dignity. Each possessed the wisdom to find purpose and meaning in the experience and rebound with greater resolve than before."

> — JANET PFEIFFER, PRES., CEO. Pfeiffer Power Seminars, LLC.
> Author of *The Secret Side of Anger*.
> www.PfeifferPowerSeminars.com

"In the past women have kept their private affairs secret and this would prevent them from breathing soulfully. This book allows contributing writers to share their experiences so that other women may be blessed and take on a new freedom in their own lives."

> — REV. DR. MARY A. TUMPKIN. President and Senior Minister of The Universal Foundation for Better Living, Inc. Author of *Before You Pray -Forgive, Tithing: Are You Ready?* and *Do You Know the Secret?: Understanding the Spiritual Nature of the Law of Attraction.*

"Sue and Kathy have created a beautiful resource in *Empowering Transformations for Women*. Thank you for sharing women's struggles and their uplifting stories. It is inspiring to read through the pages and connect with each one."

> — DEBBIE PHILLIPS, Founder, Women on Fire. Author of 2010 Indie Award® Winner Best Anthology: *Women on Fire: 20 Inspiring Women Share Their Life Secrets (and Save You Years of Struggle!)*
> www.beawomanonfire.com

" Having the courage to listen to deepest selves and then to follow our dreams, to 'sing the song of our soul' is a gift every woman deserves. *Empowering Transformations for Women* will help give you that gift! Read the book and drink up the energy, spirit, and courage that will certainly infuse you."

> —Dr. Barbara Becker Holstein, Positive Psychologist, Happiness Coach and author of *The Truth (I'm a girl, I'm smart and I know everything)*

EMPOWERING TRANSFORMATIONS
for Women

*True Stories of Purpose, Faith and Action
to Guide You Through Your Ever-Unfolding
Personal and Professional Life*

Powerful You!
PUBLISHING
NEW JERSEY USA

Empowering Transformations for Women
True Stories of Purpose, Faith and Action
To Guide You Through Your Ever-Unfolding
Personal and Professional Life

Copyright © 2011

Cover Design by Donna LaPlaca
Editor: Sheri Horn Hasan

Published by: Powerful You! Inc. NJ USA
www.powerfulyoupublishing.com

Library of Congress Control Number: 2011922522

Sue Urda and Kathy Fyler– First Edition

ISBN: 978-1-4507-5908-3

First Edition March 2011

Self Help / Women's Studies

Printed in the United States of America

Dedication

This book is dedicated
to every woman seeking her true self
and every woman assisting her journey.

"Come to the edge, he said.
They said: We are afraid.
Come to the edge, he said.
They came.
He pushed them and they flew."

~ Guillaume Apollinaire

Table of Contents

PART TWO:
TRANSFORMATION THROUGH ADVERSITY

PART THREE:
TRANSFORMATION THROUGH SPIRITUAL AWAKENING

FOREWORD

At some point in time throughout the course of our lives on earth we will come to a realization that we are intended for personal greatness, that we are fully accepted in the highest sense and that we are whole and complete. It may be in the last five minutes of our lives or it may be in the next five minutes today. The only real question before us is: "When?"

At some point while life is progressing along its course, we begin to see that the obstacles on our path, the points of pain, resistance and fear are not all bad; that within the same circumstances that we endure, we also prevail. All too often that point is on the latter side of the journey after we have suffered long enough, but occasionally we find a secret pathway that cuts through the forest more easily and a quickening occurs. We put the pieces together and we jump forward toward the joyful experience that life was intended to be.

As Grace would have it we seem to be reaching out sooner rather than later at this time in our evolution, and we find ourselves in the company of those that have "been there" and are willing to tell their stories from a perspective that sheds light on a process that we all go through in one way or another. When this happens we gain from their experience and allow ourselves to grow and awaken without having to do more of the same ourselves. We are interested in mastering the meaning of life and we are attaining it.

The process that we go through is the realization that every life event serves more than one purpose and serves on more than one dimension. It provides an opportunity to learn on the physical dimension to navigate the world in a more effective manner, to be more loving to ourselves, and to foresee ways to allow that to express more abundantly through choosing empowerment. And, it also provides us an opportunity to awaken at our spiritual dimension and very core essence level; it is a soulful journey.

The core foundation of everything in existence is energy. The bottom line essence of everything is energy. As energy vibrates at different frequencies it creates the different aspects of the physical world that we live in while on earth: all people, places and things. When we learn to manage ourselves and our lives from this energetic level, behind the scenes, we become masterful at life rather than victims to its happenings.

When we learn to choose from the subtle, invisible energetic level of life: our gut feelings, our heart space, our hunches and our inner wisdom, we begin to *create* life before it manifests under someone else's plan. Life's challenges provide us the ability to learn to do just that. We are here to realize that we can create rather than merely find the best way to react.

In this way we can begin to see that the "obstacles on our obstacle course of life" are there to allow us to muscle up in certain ways similar to the obstacle course we engage in for physical exercise: certain obstacles for certain results. They are actually put there on purpose for our highest soulful intention. On some soulful level we needed the obstacles to call us to our deepest Truth. It can be seen as a Divine collaboration that we called to us in order to awaken to our immense power.

When we are called to courage under terrifying circumstances, or called to forgive something that is nearly unforgivable, or when we are stretched in ways beyond what we thought we were capable of, we come to know ourselves in ways that we did not know existed. In this way the greatest service to the deepest part of us is done.

Does it mean we have to suffer in order to grow or to see our full potential? No.

It just happens to be a very effective way to get the job done. And interestingly I have found in the nearly 30 years of working with individuals one on one and in group settings in the area of personal development and physical and spiritual health, the suffering is directly proportional to the amount of resistance that we carry to our inherent greatness.

When we carry the illusion that we are not meant to have what we want, or that we are undeserving in some way, or if we simply have not been in the circumstance that allows us to develop our own sense of self significance, we attract circumstances that validate the absence of wholeness—the illusion.

When we resist the Truth that we are here by choice and that we are intended to navigate this experience with great mastery of faith and trust so that we can experience creative energy in action, we first will find ourselves in circumstances that seem very painful. But ultimately we will prevail, as it is our destiny.

There are of course other ways to get the job done as well, and Women's Anthology is a beautiful tool in that direction. By reading and learning from other's experiences with this conversation in mind we can utilize our imagination, our ingenuity and our own creativity to visualize our lives from the wisdom side of the obstacle course. Leap forward from other's experiences. Stand on their shoulders and allow ourselves to see further through the trees.

The caring individuals that share the authorship of these pages are aware of such perspectives. In their various avenues of arrival to this place of awareness through their various personal stories they share a piece of the Truth that is available to each of us, every day. The invitation is to read, to reflect and to remember your own true capacity with each chapter that unfolds. The encouragement thereafter is that we each move through life with an awareness that there is more than one reason for everything that is happening.

Everything that is happening is occurring to remind us of our power to choose an empowered version of response in life and also to remind us that we are made of the abundant co-creative energy that all of creation is built upon and with that to remember that we are here to create rather than simply respond.

We no longer have to create what we *don't* want in order to know what we *do* want. We can leap forward in trust that we are intended to live our heart's passion; that our personal dreams are enough; they are valid and in fact needed in the world. When we speak our truth we bring medicine to the world. Ultimately, we will realize that Creation can truly only deliver on goodness – no matter how great the challenge that is required to invite us to surrender to our greatness – only goodness shall be revealed in the end.

I offer much gratitude and celebration to the contributors of this book. Within these pages are tremendous navigational tools and examples of how we find our masterful way through the forest. And better yet, they show us examples of how to call upon the Truth that flows from our very core and to choose to see this journey as having been put in place simply for our grand adventure of awakening to the powerful co-creators that we are.

Our trip through the forest becomes a joyful calling out of our greatness. May the journey begin to deepen in the next five minutes of your life rather than your last five. But fret not, either way you get to win.

Blessings to All.

Dr. Sue Morter
www.drsuemorter.com

INTRODUCTION

What's so great about this or what's in it for me? These may be the first thoughts that cross your mind when something is placed in front of you—so you might be wondering what is between the covers of this book that you are now holding.

Or you might be wondering how a book like this comes together. More accurately, you may wish to know how a group of women from all over North America—many who don't even know each other and may never even meet in person—have conspired to bring forth such a book.

You might wonder why they would bare their souls, expose their secrets and show you their flaws.

You might ask who would share such deeply personal and sometimes unflattering truths about themselves. Who would air their 'dirty laundry' or put themselves up for possible ridicule, judgment and scrutiny? Why go there if you don't have to? Why not keep it tucked away in a closet somewhere and go on living your life?

The answer is simple…

These women have stepped into their power.

As you read the stories you will see the raw emotion and unbridled heart of each author. You will share in her joys and her pain; you will laugh, cry and celebrate with her. Her story may reflect your own, and through her transformation, you will gain insights and strength, courage and freedom.

Mostly, you may see yourself in some of these stories. These are ordinary women who have transformed their circumstances into something personally extraordinary. The evidence is in the lives they live today.

It takes a village, not only to raise a child, but to raise ourselves into the women we would have ourselves become.

It is the wish and intent of these authors to be truthful with themselves and others so that they may move forward powerfully in life, having learned and grown from their mistakes, triumphs and experiences—and if *they* can do it, *you* can too! Many of these authors have careers and businesses that focus on assisting other women to empower themselves, and all of them have chosen to share their story in the hopes of helping someone like you along the way.

It is said that you must first release the past before you can fully live the potential for your life. I believe this to be true.

Allow yourself to become immersed in the stories and learn the lessons that are shared through their words—they may help you to move forward from the circumstances or beliefs that hold you back. In these stories you will find comfort, guidance and joy. And surely you will find hope.

May you also find personal meaning for yourself in these pages, and may the stories of these authors serve as a beacon of strength for your journey.

It is our intention and purpose to be a source for good and to do our part in raising consciousness and compassion in the world one person at a time. This book and these authors book contribute greatly to this purpose.

Know above all that you can be, do and have anything you desire. These women are living proof. And if you ever need encouragement or inspiration - flip through the book, open a page and read. Your heart will open and expand.

Blessings and Success to You, You Powerful Woman!

Sue Urda
www.sueurda.com

PART ONE

Transformation
Through
Self-Discovery

*"I will realize my own worth when I realize
I am the most valuable thing that I have in life."
~ Iyanla Vanzant*

Learning to Live in Balance
Denise Abda

I'd dropped twenty-three pounds in four weeks and felt like there was something crawling under my skin. I experienced diarrhea, intense pain behind my eyes, and I craved clay. Yet no doctor could tell me what was wrong!

It was May 1988 as I began my journey to live a better life. At that time, I'd worked for the past ten years in a local hospital, testing other people's blood to help determine the causes of their illnesses.

Yet when I tested my own blood, I could find nothing wrong. Despite following my doctors' orders, I continued to lose weight quickly and felt nauseous all the time. The terrible cravings continued and, when my teeth felt loose one day in June, I knew I was becoming malnourished because my system was not absorbing any nutrients.

And still every one of my blood tests, X-rays, CT scans and other diagnostic tests came back normal, yet my symptoms persisted. Why was I so sick and continuing to fail? Why couldn't the medical professionals find the answers to my problem?

I began to question traditional medical practices and the work I was doing as a professional in the medical field. I questioned the fact that when I tested the blood of patients diagnosed with fourth stage liver cancer, the tests showed liver enzymes within normal limits. Something is wrong with this methodology, I thought.

I had symptoms of irritable bowel syndrome, Crohn's disease or ulcerative colitis, but these diagnostic tests all came back negative. That just didn't make sense to me.

Finally, my search led me to a prevention medicine doctor in New York City. Desperate, I felt it was my last resort, and I made the appointment with high hopes. Within three weeks of following his recommended dietary changes, adding supplements, and understanding what nutritional therapy was about, I felt better and my symptoms calmed down.

As I was feeling better I began to seek out books on nutrition and medicine. One in particular, "What Your Doctor Didn't Learn in Medical School," covered much of what this new doctor had taught me. More books on nutrition opened my eyes further: extra Vitamin A for this, zinc helps that, essential fats, B-complex, minerals—they're all good for something, but the key is to keep them all in proper balance.

As I continued to learn many dietary theories, I came across the work of Dr. Robert O. Young at the ph Miracle Center in San Diego. His research about the importance of an alkaline lifestyle and balance to achieve better health fascinated me...let's see...the world is in balance: night/day, up/down, in/out, warm/cold, sick/health, acid/alkaline...I needed to investigate!

The friend who'd enlightened me about this work said, "Dr. Young's research had turned leukemia around in seventy-two hours." Of course, I didn't believe it. If it was true, why wasn't it headline news, and why don't we all know about it?

Only the Beginning

It's here that my real story begins. The more I read his work, the more I sought answers. I decided to enroll in his class about live cell microscopy. With a background in blood testing, I knew this was going to be interesting...

Ten days before I was all set to travel across the country to California, my mother was diagnosed with acute myelogenous leukemia (AML.) In AML, the bone marrow releases immature white blood cells called blasts. In a diagnosed leukemia patient, they have not developed enough and are now in the blood prematurely. However, when blasts are found in a leukemia profile, something has to be done quickly because time is of the essence. These cells will quickly crowd out normal red cell production, healthy white blood cells and platelets that the body needs daily.

I discovered this news in the local laboratory where I worked. How odd was that? I'd been told that the work coming from the pH Miracle center reversed leukemia within seventy-two hours, and now my mom is diagnosed with the same disease! Why did my friend specifically say "leukemia," and not some kind of cancer? It seemed so unreal to me.

I knew from a conventional stand point that her blood was fifty percent leukemic, and if I didn't get her into the hospital and under the care of a doctor, she only had a few days to live. I rushed home and called the ph Miracle center. Amazingly, Dr. Young was passing by when the phone rang and answered my call.

After a brief discussion of my mother's situation, he proceeded to educate me about how to change the way we look at this disease. He told me, "Your mother is an undiagnosed celiac and not making any blood, so now her body has to send white blood cells out into circulation, and that is what they call leukemia. The medical doctors only know how to poison the cells to kill them, and that will also kill her. She needs to start making her own red blood cells again and her white blood cell count will come down."

Frightened, I was unsure if I should follow the advice of this nutrition scientist, researcher and naturopath who I hadn't even heard of until three months ago. I really didn't know much about him and his theories, and he was literally across the country.

I immediately ordered the products and supplements designed to reduce acid and help get her back into an alkaline state of health. They arrived overnight. The following evening, after taking these nutritional products, my mother did not have her night sweats, nor did she have that hacking cough she'd developed over the past two to three weeks.

She even felt better the next morning. So, I thought, something must be right here. But, still I was fearful and didn't want to upset her, and if something happened, I would never forgive myself for not getting some professional help at hand.

So, she went into the hospital, by her decision, to be treated conventionally. The treatment for AML at the time consisted of chemotherapy infusion constantly for one week. I asked the doctor if I could help her through this by treating her from a nutritional standpoint. He had no problem with it. I began by using aloe vera, and gave her alkaline water all day long. I supplied her with supplements that I understood to be helpful, and pureed food, because I wanted her to get the most benefit to heal and save her energy in order to overcome this terrible "blood cancer."

Then, I read in the book "Sick & Tired" by Dr. Young that leukemia is not cancer at all; it's the body's inability to make red blood cells. He says the reality is that the physical body is sending out immature white blood cells from the bone marrow to compensate for not making any red blood cells.

So what does conventional medicine do? They kill these white blood cells with chemo, along with killing everything else. Now, I know, *not* a good idea to help someone diagnosed with this condition. She needed to balance herself in order to make healthy red blood cells, so her bone marrow would stop pushing the immature white blood cells out into circulation. In other words, get with the cause and stop treating the symptoms.

She went through the chemotherapy; I threw away the hospital food, and traveled back and forth with pureed alkaline food because the villi of her small intestinal tract were impaired and not absorbing nutrients. Therefore, she could not make red blood cells. She lived on green soups, healing soups, smoothies, and only took her meds with alkaline water.

An infection control specialist came in and wondered why she didn't have any fevers, no open sores, no chills, no spleen enlargement, not the typical case of AML for a woman of her age. Little did they know I was working very hard with non-conventional modalities: energy medicine techniques; Ayurveda, EFT; Reiki, a mycodetox supplement; prayer, and *A Course in Miracles*, to name a few—it was the least I could do.

At one point, her oncologist asked me what I was giving her. I told him some supplements and aloe vera. He looked perplexed. I was afraid to say I knew something he didn't know, and was working with the research of alkaline balanced health. This was my mother and I wanted the best available option.

She'd made it through the initial treatment and came home to be treated on an outpatient basis. "How bittersweet" I overheard the doctor say to his nurse on our way out. I was glad to be out of the hospital environment.

After three months, mom was stable enough for me to head out to the ph Miracle center and work with the class I'd intended to take before her diagnosis. When I returned home, I told my mom that now I really knew what to do for her. I understand what health is and how to achieve it.

A short time later, she was erroneously administered a flu shot. Immuno-compromised, her body didn't need another thing to fight, and she succumbed to its effects and passed shortly thereafter.

I look back at this time in my life as my "ah-ha" moment. I know now it all happened for a greater purpose. I'd been given the tools to understand health and healing in a new light, and I know that you can't heal something unless you consider the cause.

I knew this was *my* wake-up call; consciousness is right at our fingertips, but we're not paying attention. I learned the importance of energy balance, consciousness, transitioning and alternative therapies.

Both our illnesses were a call for action. I searched to find answers to make a difference in her treatment because I knew what would happen to her when treated conventionally, and in this process, I learned to live in balance, seek and trust a higher truth. Now, I use this to help others. The answers are available, and it helps when you pay attention to the resources that present themselves to you.

ABOUT THE AUTHOR: Denise promotes her mission to help people achieve optimal health through education, knowledge, understanding and awareness through her work as a health consultant. Armed with a BS in Biochemistry from the University of Scranton, Pennsylvania, certification by the American Society of Clinical Pathology (ASCP) and in Microscopy from the pH Miracle Center in San Diego. Previously employed at Community Medical Center in Scranton as a Medical Technologist, Denise also graduated from The Institute of Integrative Nutrition in NYC and earned certification from The American Association of Drugless Practitioners (AADP.)

Denise Abda, MT(ASCP), IMA, HC(AADP)
Summit Balance
YpHBalance@yahoo.com
570-586-9166

Laugh, Love, Live
Lora Colautti

Just a few days after Christmas, exhausted from traveling more than thirty hours, I arrived home from my amazing five-week trip to Australia. As my dad greeted me at the local airport he broke the news that changed my life forever.

My younger sister, best friend, and only sibling Andrea was diagnosed with breast cancer while I was away. She was thirty and first noticed symptoms while breast feeding her second child.

After months of chemo therapy, a bilateral mastectomy, and radiation, the cancer found its way into her spinal and brain fluid. Fourteen months after her diagnosis, with loving family by her side, she passed away. Her amazingly powerful and positive journey through her illness and passing is a beautiful and inspiring story.

But that's not the story I'm going to tell. The story I have to tell begins earlier. It begins on my thirtieth birthday.

The Awakening

The day I turned thirty years old I made a choice, a commitment to myself. It was one that I practiced in the years following and one that ultimately helped me to see the beauty and inspiration in my sister's short journey from diagnosis to death.

As I lay in the warm summer sun that day, before friends and family came to join me in my birthday celebration, I reflected upon where I had been and where I wanted to go. I asked myself what I wanted the next thirty years of my life to be like. Did I want to continue my current state of over analyzing and being stuck in my head? Did my concern with what *others* thought I should do truly serve me?

The words: "I will only make choices that feel good to me" resonated from deep down in my gut. When I said the words out loud, they sounded so right…Little did I know that such a simple statement would ultimately have such a profound effect.

And so began my new way of living. Every time I made a choice about something, I became conscious of how I handled it. Instead of analyzing every problem or decision, I allowed myself to consider which path, which choice *felt* best? I began to make decisions that came from my heart and center instead of my head.

Shortly after my thirtieth birthday the opportunity presented itself for me to become a self-employed sales rep for a home party company. While I'd never done anything like this before, I recognized that the old me would have allowed other people's opinions to make up much of my decision. What *they* thought—*their* worry and doubt on my behalf—determined my course of action far more than how I felt about any given situation.

And although for a brief fleeting moment my head urged me to play it safe and keep doing the same things I was already doing, I started to pay less attention to both what those around me had to say and my own self-defeating thoughts. As I allowed myself to focus instead on how I *felt*, I realized I was being presented with an exciting and challenging opportunity that just might lead to major growth!

I never would have taken that leap of faith and made such a drastic change if I'd continued to listen to the voices outside of myself. But when I tuned in to my "inner voice," I acted from a new place, a place of strength, a place that enabled me to enter a new and exciting phase of my life.

It was this decision to "go within" that proved invaluable during my sister's illness and passing. Through my ability to make *feeling* choices and to take a conscious look at the positives around me, I was able to inspire others to do the same. By staying connected to my true self I was able to be present and helpful for my family and—most importantly—for my sister.

Even though she was an encouraging and up lifting person by nature, there were nonetheless times during her illness when Andrea needed others to inspire her. Emotionally and physically exhausted from chemo treatments and the myriad of other drugs she took, there were times when she found it difficult to stay positive and maintain her usual "I'm going to kick cancer's ass!" attitude.

Rather than get caught up in the negative thoughts circulating through my head, I pondered what action would feel best for both me and Andrea.

I knew I couldn't take the cancer away from her or make the treatments stop, but I could try to help her feel just a little bit better. So I made her a music CD with songs of inspiration, excitement, and fun—songs to help her regain her "kick butt" attitude. It was a small act, but one that came from a place of love, hope, and good feeling thoughts. Every time she listened to it, it helped her feel just a little bit better. And I felt better too.

I knew that if I'd gotten caught up in her pain and frustration, I wouldn't have been able to help her or myself. Rather than focus on the disheartening details of my sister's current realities, I chose to empower us both by doing something that allowed us to simply be in the moment and *feel*.

I realize now that whenever I'd look at the situation outside of myself, I'd feel as if I had no control. I saw that I—before the epiphany on my thirtieth birthday—so many times had felt disempowered in my own life. And it was that feeling of lack of control that caused me to experience fear, frustration, self-doubt, and sadness.

Although the end result of my sister's cancer journey was not at all the outcome we'd hoped for, through it all I know I did my best. I learned to tap into my emotions and, in doing so, I was able to be more present and more joyful in the moments that I had left with her, my sister, my best friend.

Moving On

Shortly after Andrea passed away, my passion as a home party consultant began to fade. My spirit knew it was time for a change.

As I sat, waiting quietly for an inspiration from the universe, the words "life coach" came to me in a flash. Years ago, I would have thought about it logically. I would have asked myself: Are life coach's really successful? Can I afford the schooling? Who am *I* to think I can help others?

But the new, connected me knew better. By the next day I had made the decision to become a life coach. As I registered for my first course and announced my departure from the home party business there were no second guesses, no analyzing or worry. It just felt right!

I knew that making choices from my gut, my heart, and the good feeling place of my center, was all I needed to do. After so many years of putting it into practice I truly believed it was making a difference in my life.

A few years later—after a lot of positive decision making and coaching courses—I not only became a certified life coach and created my own coaching business called Purposeful Life Coaching, I also met my man.

You know the one. He gets me, supports me, encourages me, communicates with me, makes me laugh, makes me smile, and makes my toes curl! I'd been single for nearly seven years and, with my new found commitment to trust my feelings, happily so. I filled my life with *me*—my friends and my experiences.

And now that I knew, without a doubt, who I was and the type of guy I wanted to connect with, I was ready for a relationship, but not just any relationship.

Over the years, the total number of my first dates could have formed a sports team! They were all nice, but none of them *felt* right. As excited as I was to be meeting new people, the "it" factor just wasn't there—until I met Andy.

I noticed him every time he came into the store where I worked. It was as though a spotlight shone down on him. Definitely not like any of the other guys I had met! His bright smile and eyes sent butterflies fluttering through me whenever I was near him. Although I was curious about him, I didn't act on my interest. For whatever reason, something in my gut told me the time wasn't right.

Then everything changed the day before Christmas.

I went to work that day dressed as an elf, wearing striped socks, an elf hat with bells and my cheeks painted red. He came into the store, and when I looked at him, the imaginary spotlight was shining down "highlighting" him more than ever!

He looked at me with a smile I will never forget. His eyes seemed to sparkle as he asked me for a Christmas hug. As we embraced, careful not to smear my red painted elf cheeks, I felt an energy and connection I'd never felt with any other man. My brain swirled with curiosity, as my heart began to pound, and my spirit danced.

The "elf hug" was only the beginning. My heart sings every time I'm with him. After living the single life for seven years, this relationship is a wonderful way to continue my commitment—not only to myself but to my partner—to lead from my good feeling place…always.

In all areas of my life, including this relationship, I continue to make choices based on what feels good to me.

When I spoke at my sister's funeral, I emphasized how important it is to embrace and enjoy life. "We've all heard the saying 'live, love, laugh'". Now turn it around…Because when you are laughing and loving you *truly* are living. And that's what my sister's life—what all of our lives—are about. *Living."*

I keep her memory close as I move forward in life. More than ever, I stay conscious of my own feelings and continue to make choices from my place of center. I continue to "laugh, love, and live" just as I was always meant to do…

ABOUT THE AUTHOR: Lora Colautti is a natural up lifter and a certified life coach. When her sister passed away from breast cancer, Lora was able to find the joy, beauty and positives even in a heartbreaking experience. Through her coaching she now helps and supports others in doing the same in their lives. She encourages those she meets to draw inspiration from life's experiences and use it to help them move forward, filling their life with joy and purpose. Lora shares her ideas, tools and words of inspiration through coaching her clients as well as in newsletters, public speaking, seminars and workshops.

Lora Colautti, CTACC
Purposeful Life Coaching
www.alittleplc.com
Lora@alittleplc.com ~ 519-979-2027

The Hero in My Life

A Story of Transformation Through Strength and Courage
Marta Torres Cuminotto

Today, I forgave my mother and my perpetrators. Today, I fully embrace and accept the little girl who'd been hurting for years. I have no words—nothing more to say or to discuss; to reveal or to confess; to understand or to accept. Today, I came to the light, and became whole. Today was the beginning of my transformation. Today I declare myself…The Hero in My life…

The Men

I didn't know this man's name at the time. I know now he was Man Number One. This man offered the seed that gave life to the embryo that became me. I do not know him well.

Man Number Two was number one's brother. Throughout my life this man exuded only love. My earliest recollection was breakfast time one bright summer day when I was about one and a half years old. The tall slender silhouette of Man Number Two transmitted peace and calm.

Man Number Three was a young curious family member who—in need of some diversion—made me feel dirty one day while we visited his mother; while Man Number Four was a sick drunkard that became my mother's live-in boyfriend, and the one who robbed me of my innocence.

Man Number Five beat me so badly with a belt I could barely breathe through my loud cries. Wow! I can't believe the tears welling up just from the memory.

By the time Man Number Six and I were through, I was broken into many little pieces, carrying in my womb his seed.

From Man Number Six I gave birth to Man Number Seven. I fell in love with Number Seven the moment the nurse placed the little bundle in my arms. I was struck by his deep, dark eyes and brown, silky skin. Why can't I fight the tears that now run down my face as images flicker through my mind with lightening speed? Perhaps it's because of the loneliness I felt back then. Maybe the tears are just validation of a traumatic event that I've not re-visited for more than thirty years. The Event was one of the darkest times of my life. Number Seven became the reason for everything. The reason for every movement and every decision made henceforth. He became the most important man in my life. He remains until this day Beautiful Man Number Seven.

Man Number Eight was like an apparition. Swiftly, he snuck into my life with a strong grip that would not let go. This handsome, bright, funny, yet complicated man started as a mild summer day that culminated in a destructive tornado. He came out of nowhere, swept through my life with no warning, and left my emotions scattered about like the letters of a scrabble game thrown about forcefully by a toddler in play.

There were other men. However, time and space only allow me to expound on so many details and emotions. I confess, however, the lessons were life-changing and the outcome absolutely miraculous. Today, as I share two powerful incidents—about two men—I can say I believe in miracles.

Going Back

A clear blue sky and hot sun made for a beautiful day on this Caribbean island. In the background, the constant thunderous waves crash against the monster rocks behind them. I loved to follow my grandmother wherever she went, and that day was like all the others, except for what I would soon experience. As I look back, I'm reminded how little children in play mode are oblivious to how—in an instant—their lives can change from happy to devastated. I'm also reminded that adults—with their many challenges and issues—forget they are protectors of children. Equally oblivious, they are often the reason why the life of a child can change forever in an instant.

My uncle comes to visit his mother that morning. I am in the bathroom, taking a little longer than usual. My grandmother calls me and I respond. "I'm coming!" I keep saying, hurrying it up as much as I can. Then I hear my uncle's voice calling me. Now I am scared. It's the tone of his voice that starts my adrenaline rush. By the time I'm finished and out of the bathroom, walking towards the living room, the adrenaline rush is forgotten and I'm back to my happy self.

Suddenly, as forceful as a gust of wind in a storm, my attacker pounces toward me like a bulldog. I wiggle and squirm, trying to avoid the inevitable object that resembles a snake about to leash venom upon its prey. My uncle's belt, all over my skinny body, curls up as each strike leaves behind a swollen piece of my skin. He screams at me ruthlessly, "WHEN SOMEONE CALLS YOU, YOU COME RIGHT AWAY, YOU HEAR ME? RIGHT AWAY!" I could barely breathe, only horrible wails and shrills escape my mouth so painful is the ordeal.

I am left inconsolable, confused, and totally exhausted. I never forgot that day, or Man Number Five. I never forgot my feelings and emotions, or my questions, which still remain unasked and unanswered.

I now understand that episodes in our lives, along with our many experiences and emotions—however painful—find a way of hiding somewhere in our bodies, and allow us to continue to live without dying of hurt or a broken spirit. This absolutely astounds me! I find that it is one of the most miraculous processes with which our bodies have been endowed.

As I contemplate how marvelous our bodies are designed, I remain in awe. It's so interesting to know that emotions also stay dormant within us. They remain as intricately carved grooves, or impressions, in our electrical circuitry until some future stimuli awakens them.

As I sit here and write, I cry, for I realize what a terrible injustice took place that day. Most importantly, I am aware of the betrayal by those who—entrusted with my protection—chose to perpetrate such violence. For the first time since that violent act took place, I cry as I share this episode of my life, and I cannot believe how far I've traveled on the Road to Recovery.

I have no recollection whether or not my grandmother came to my rescue that day or if she tried to comfort me. What I do remember clearly is the utter loneliness I felt as I wondered; where was my protector? However, the million dollar question that surged forth again and again was, "What did I do that merited such violence?" Today, I have the answers to all my questions. Today I am free.

The Unforgettable

The incident I am about to relate took place on a cold, snowy, winter night in the City Of Brotherly Love—Philadelphia. I was terrified to get in the family car. I look out the window, only to see the car sliding, sometimes to the left and sometimes to the right. Like a mummy displayed upright in a museum, I am stiff with fear, my arms hold my stomach tightly as I wait for something awful to happen. My mother argues with Man Number Four, who slurs his words, and looks and smells disgusting. Thank God we arrive home safely.

I never felt comfortable in his presence. I didn't trust him. The way he moved his lips and the words and phrases he chose, made me feel ashamed. It all started gradually. It was confusing and I could not escape it. I wish I had a protector to spare me from this nightmare. The event would haunt me for decades. The event transported me to another part of my mind in order to survive. Since that event, I was never again able to be one hundred percent present in my life. I never told anyone.

Years later, I'm raising my twelve year old son, whose behavior is becoming increasingly unbearable. I also notice that every morning upon arising I have a sick feeling in my stomach that affects my entire body. Getting up to go to work becomes increasingly difficult. One day at work I cry uncontrollably, and ask myself, what's happening with me? My boss suggests I see a professional to help me sort through what's going on and, for the first time in my life, I consult a therapist.

When I share the details of my son's behavior with the therapist, I'm surprised at his answer and subsequent questions. His words still ring in my ears as I travel back in time to that day. "I think what you have described is a normal twelve year old boy, Marta. But tell me, how are YOU feeling? Why don't we talk about YOU today?" My long road to recovery from childhood sexual abuse begins.

In time, I accepted the fact that, all along, I blamed my mother for the abuse that took place many years ago, and I understood the feelings of estrangement that resulted on my part. Through this process, I discovered that when a child is robbed of their innocence at such an early age, feelings of guilt, shame, lack of self-esteem, and self-worth keep them from developing into emotionally and mentally healthy adults—qualities needed for success and achievement in life. Until they explore their hurtful past and put the pieces together, they cannot become the "whole" people they are intended to be.

The sick feelings in my stomach were a direct consequence of the disgusting events which no child should ever have to experience. For decades, these flashes of my past would haunt me and condemn me day in and day out. With the help of books and recommended courses, along with changes in my personal daily habits, I was able to come out of that darkness.

Epilogue

This loving professional became the first man in a very long time I could trust. With his help, I broke the ice and began to feel comfortable with myself and my relationship with men. A true professional in his field, I bless the day I found him.

Eight years have passed since that first visit to him. I now sit in front of a woman I've been seeing for the past year. This would be my last visit with Helene, the second true professional in her field. My mother passed away a few months ago. She was the topic of most of our conversations. Today I encountered the Power of

Unconditional Love, the Power of Forgiveness, and the Power of Acceptance.

ABOUT THE AUTHOR: Marta's mission to make a difference in the way women perceive themselves stems from her ability to triumph over traumatic life events. Since 2002, she's poured her entrepreneurial spirit into an exclusive hair removal practice for women and girls. Marta's strength and courage enabled her to discover—and embrace—the special person hidden behind the pain that haunted her for years. Through her writing, Marta shares with others her secrets of survival as she continues through her transformational journey. Marta currently provides Healthy Living Presentations to inspire women toward their own transformational process through self care.

Marta Torres Cuminotto
Absolutely Permanent Hair Removal, LLC
www.absolutelynohair.com
marta@nohair.comastbiz.net
203-913-1189

The Dream Stealers
RoseMarie Couture DeSaro

The thumping sound grew louder. Someone was coming! Quick, pretend you're asleep!

Downstairs in Linda's basement, where she and I had spent most of the night giggling and snacking, we ducked under the covers on the pull-out sofa bed when we heard the sound of her father descending the stairs.

"Oh boy, he's gonna be mad we're still up," Linda whispered as she scrunched her eyes shut and disappeared under the blanket. I lay next to her, quiet and still.

When her father finished making his way down the rickety staircase, he approached my side of the bed. Without saying a word, I watched through slit eyes as he slid his pants zipper down and something poked out. Before my ten year old brain could process what was happening, he reached down to grasp my hand, which lay outside the covers.

With my other hand, I desperately tried to poke Linda under the covers. She did not respond. How she could have fallen asleep?! What do I do, I don't want him to touch me! Panicked, I kept poking and pushing Linda until finally I either hurt her or annoyed her, she grunted "stop it!" and then rolled over to face the other side of the bed. Quickly, her father disappeared back up the stairs.

The next day I knew I had to do something. But talking to my brother and sisters was out of the question—I was the youngest of five and as it was they teased me constantly. I had zero communication with my parents when it came to anything remotely emotional. My dad was in the bottle in his own little world most of the time, and my Mom, well she just didn't seem to know how to openly express her emotions. A product of their own upbringings, both of my parents passively promoted keeping the door to emotions shut airtight.

So I told Linda what happened, assuming she would believe me and find a way to make it all right. But what occurred after that only made it worse—so much worse...

I remember the day like yesterday, though by now approximately forty-four years have passed. I was summoned in front of her father, who sat in his arm chair, his wife behind him with her hand supportively on his shoulder, and my friend Linda sitting closely in front of him on the floor. They looked like the perfect family portrait.

"Who the hell do you think you are, little girl, making up such disgusting and filthy stories?" he shouted at me from the sanctuary of his chair. "Don't you know that you can go to jail for telling such horrible lies?"

"I've got a good mind to call the police on you right now! From now on, you'd better learn how to behave when you come into this house, and don't you ever lie again about what goes on here or I'll have them come and lock you up for good!" My friend and her mother remained silent the whole time. Mortified, I went home and never told another soul.

Nothin' But Trouble

After that, trouble seemed to follow me consistently. Particularly trouble with men...by the time I was a little older, I found myself dodging sexual advances left and right. The loving husband next door, a schoolmate's dirty old grandfather, and even a brother-in-law (now an ex-brother in law!) seemed hell bent on cornering me in one way or another.

One routine Sunday Italian family dinner stands out the most. I could smell the meatballs and gravy cooking in the kitchen (in Brooklyn its gravy, not sauce!) The house was full of family members all talking loudly over one another. The TV blasted the football game, Dad cussed the

Jets, grandmother and mom drank Manhattans, and I—a typical sixteen year old—had retreated to my upstairs bedroom for some peace and quiet.

Suddenly, the door flung open and in my brother-in-law strutted with his pants down around his ankles. I guess he thought he was bringing me some kind of gift! I quickly shoved him out of my room and slammed the door closed. Again, I kept it to myself.

It's no wonder by the time I turned sweet sixteen, I knew how to manipulate men. Defining my success in male terms, I decided I'd be the first in my family to attend college, to work at a super successful career, and I'd bear children at a later age. I made it my mission to prove that a woman could accomplish anything a man could do. Not such remarkable goals for today's young females, but I established this life plan in 1973!

Shortly after college I was introduced to lifting free weights. It made me feel sexy, strong and confident. I decided to compete professionally and to undertake it as a career. Unfortunately, I quickly learned how many people thrive on discouraging a pioneer or visionary. Told I was already too old, I'd have to move to California, etc., and filled with uncertainty, I listened to the dream stealers and gave up the dream.

Working Girl

A pro at guarding myself against both sexual advances and emotional outbreaks at this point in my life, Wall Street seemed the natural next stop for me. Ironically, I knew that my Brooklyn wise-guy sense of humor, bodybuilding experience, and emotional coolness, placed me on level footing with any man out there.

Six years later I became the first female regional marketing director of my ultra conservative firm on Wall Street. I broke the glass ceiling, crashed the boy's party, and I did it on my terms!

Then the stock market crash of 1987 derailed my perfect plan. Forced to seek out new opportunities, I began a network marketing direct sales career in 1989.I garnered significant success my first year, but when the industry took a beating I lost my confidence, listened again to the dream stealers, and walked away. I didn't have enough belief in myself to allow entrepreneurship to expose my weaknesses. I felt far safer under the corporate umbrella.

The next ten plus years were a mix of on again, off again business opportunities, intertwined with corporate America. I experienced successes and failures alike. Through it all, I still felt more confident with the safety net of a corporate environment.

And then the unthinkable happened. On an early September crystal blue sky day, I was running late and thinking *there has to be a better way*. I rushed to catch the 8:47 a.m. boat, and witnessed the first plane crash into One World Trade Center.

I never made it into my building. I saw my secretary crying for her sister, and while consoling her we saw the second plane coming and ran into the park. It was a moment of sheer panic as terror gripped us; a defining moment when you get to know *exactly* who you are.

While others fled to get to their boat and escape, knocking people down en route, I climbed the park benches looking for my brother, nephew, brother-in-law, and friends.

Cell phones didn't work. I let several boats come and go. The barge on which we stood was not meant for so many people and began to rock fiercely. People panicked and yelled to the deckhand to close the gates and leave others behind.

I was appalled but decided it would be smarter to cross the Hudson River to the Jersey side. There I found a ghost town; the buildings normally bustling with people were now destitute. It was then the first building fell and I knew it was time to go home. I watched the second tower fall in my car's rearview mirror. The highway was a twilight zone, not a soul around, only some abandoned cars.

This day turned out to be a pivotal moment in my life in more ways than one, though I had yet to learn exactly how.

The Drive of a Lamborghini

A few years later, the entrepreneurial failures overshadowed the corporate successes. I once took a psychological test that concluded I had the drive of a Lamborghini. But where was my drive now, and for what? What was it about the safety of the corporate environment that prevented me from going it alone? Where did the powerful, fearless, confident, determined woman go?

I knew it was time to carefully reevaluate my life. Then I attended a company sponsored intense five day life changing event, where I learned we are all born to win and then programmed to lose! As part of the training, I relived the incident of sexual abuse from forty-four years ago. While I'd always known it affected my relationships with men, I never realized how much I censored myself emotionally because of the fear instilled in me during that early episode with my friend's father, compounded by discouragement of emotional expression during my early family life.

That threat had subconsciously paved the road to my lack of confidence. Along with learning to keep a lid on my emotions, I stifled my natural *confident* instinct for survival. This set me up to succeed only when I had the confidence of a concrete safety net.

I started asking myself the right questions. I learned that my strength, courage and resiliency were innate, and that only second guessing myself made me vulnerable to what others said or thought. That day on 9/11, I understood that God had given me these traits to learn how to survive. It was only my limiting beliefs that held me back from the life about which I'd always dreamed.

Finally able to deal with it and move on, I now understood the wall that protects me from disappointment also separates me from my dream, the past does not equal the future, and nobody can shake my confidence without my permission. Back to life again, I reclaimed my power!

Epilogue

The ringing phone startled me out of deep thought. Amazingly, it was my childhood friend Linda. After catching up on all that had transpired over the past twenty-five years, I turned the subject to her father. How could I not? Her call was just too coincidental!

She told me she'd struggled with truth and fiction her whole life, but that her mother had always believed my story about that night. Suddenly, I felt at peace. The last of the dream stealers banished, I said goodbye to Linda and set about to rock my entrepreneurial world with confidence!

ABOUT THE AUTHOR: An "on and off" entrepreneur for the past 21 years, Roe DeSaro began her career in the corporate arena on Wall Street. She quickly broke several "class ceilings," most notably becoming the first female, non-stockbroker, to become vice president & regional director of marketing & sales for a prominent firm. It was during the "mergers & acquisition" era on Wall Street that Roe began her entrepreneurial missions. Today she runs a successful home-based business for a lifestyle company that markets travel-centric products. From Bond broker, to Stockbroker to FunBroker, she is creating more fun, freedom, and fulfillment in other people's lives.

RoseMarie Couture DeSaro
FunBroker Benefits & Co.
Roe@funNwealth.com
732.673.1763

A Brave New World

Barbara Molnar Dunne

My mom wasn't too crazy about Bob entering my world. She liked life just the way it was—the two of us together. At my age, I guess she'd never envisioned that I might someday actually get married.

Single and in my fifties, mom and I lived together in our townhome on Staten Island. Day after day, I traveled on the X12 express bus from Staten Island to midtown Manhattan, where I worked as an executive assistant. And at the end of each day I returned to mom.

As time had passed and I'd remained single, we'd decided to share households. This made perfectly good sense to us both, since we'd always gotten along well and spent a lot of our free time together. However, I didn't realize until the years had drifted past that many of our relatives began to consider us a "couple." Invitations to weddings, christenings, communions, anniversaries and other parties would come addressed to us both, rather than to each of us with a guest. I took note of it, but I guess it never really bothered me, until...

Bob, one of the bus operators on the X12, used to chat with me when I sat up front. He'd tell me about his two sons and their wives, and he beamed when he spoke of his grandchildren. Distinctive looking with a long gray ponytail and full moustache, he always had a kindly look in his green eyes.

One day we talked about how much we both wanted to see an exhibit at the Metropolitan Museum of Art, and agreed we'd go sometime. Several weeks later it came to pass. While the antique gun collection excited Bob (and me too, actually!), I was ecstatic to see some of my favorite Impressionists' paintings.

It was amazing how relaxed I felt that day. Quite a while since I last dated, I was less concerned about making a good impression than I was about simply having a nice day together. I just wanted to live in the present and be myself. Neither of us needed to be perfect.

We walked through Central Park, sat a while, and walked some more. You couldn't ask for a prettier spring day. Before we knew it, we reached Columbus Circle. Famished, I remembered a French bistro not far from there that I'd enjoyed in the past.

I didn't know if Bob liked French food or not, but even if he didn't he was very accommodating. When the waiter set down his plate with five scallops, three asparagus spears, and a dollop of mashed potatoes, we looked at each other and burst out laughing. Bob's a hefty guy with an appetite to match, and that portion was really just a "snack" for him.

As we continued to talk and laugh, and enjoy each other's company, it became clear we were both having a wonderful time. Our friendship grew from that point on. But now that Bob had entered my life, my relationship with my mother grew strained. Although she was cordial, my mother disliked several things about Bob. Clearly from another generation, my mother's tastes had been formed in another era and she had great difficulty understanding that much had changed over time. In some ways she was just plain old fashioned.

My Turn Now

"What's with the ponytail?" she'd complain. "He's in his fifties!" She disapproved of the fact that Bob owned a motorcycle, and that he hunted. "You mean he owns a gun?" she gasped when she found out. But her major issue was with the fact that Bob was divorced. I reminded her that his divorce occurred many years ago, that things had changed, and that if he wasn't divorced, I would never have gone out with him.

Nevertheless, when Bob came into my life, my mother began to treat me as though I was fifteen again. And, just as any normal fifteen year-old would, I resented it terribly. I know she was trying to protect me in her own way, but I didn't need protection. I reminded her on several occasions of my real age and that I knew what I was doing. We had many heart-to-heart talks, but more than a few ended with one of us walking away angry.

Throughout her life, my mother had never lived alone. The oldest of six, she married at the age of 25, and bore three children. She worked in clerical positions way into her seventies until her vision became a problem. She made it to her eighties before she felt unsafe going out alone.

When Bob and I started spending many of our weekends together, I struggled with guilt. Was I supposed to feel badly about spending so much time with him? If I didn't, how else would I get to know him? My mother had married, raised a family...wasn't it *my* turn?

"What do *I* want and deserve to have in *my* life?" I asked myself. If my relationship with Bob was leading toward marriage, I wasn't going to stop it because of my *mother!* Was I supposed to be her companion for the rest of *her* life? Besides, my mom was not a selfish woman and I knew she sincerely wanted me to have what's best for me...

In the middle of that year, after a routine annual mammogram, mom found out that she needed a lumpectomy. The pathology results were very good, and the doctors recommended radiation and drug therapy. But mom decided on drug therapy only, which she pursued only for about a year.

Visits to the oncologist always made her so nervous, and her elevated blood pressure proved it. She absolutely hated going to these appointments. I reassured her that, at her tender age of 85, if she didn't want to go, she didn't have to. After all, she should give herself a break, I told her. She seemed genuinely appreciative of my caring response and clearly felt much better after our conversations.

In October 2007 Bob and I surprised everyone and announced that we'd gotten married in a simple City Hall ceremony. Dinner with friends and family followed a few weeks later. Thankfully, mom finally began to accept that Bob's intentions were real, that he truly did love me, and that he was willing to prove it by making our relationship permanent.

At the same time I became Bob's wife, I took on the role of stepmother and step-*grand*mother. How amazing it was for me to suddenly be part of a family with children! Although we don't see the grandchildren often, we speak to them as much as we can.

I moved into Bob's apartment fifteen minutes away because the townhome I shared with my mom wasn't large enough for the three of us to be comfortable. Since I wasn't working full time, I spent as much time as I could with mom to help her through the transition. Both my brothers live out of town, in Chicago and Rome, respectively, and they call her often, but I've always been the one responsible for her well being as the years have rolled by.

The Scent of Fragrant Pines Calls Us Home

While dating, Bob had brought me up to his house in Maine. He'd purchased it long before he met me—after visiting friends for a hunting weekend he'd fallen in love with the house next door that turned out to be for sale. The price was right, so he'd made an offer to buy it.

Two months later he was a homeowner. Since it's a ten hour trip from New York City, and Bob had only five weeks' vacation time, the house remained empty most of the time. Bob planned to make a permanent move there when he retired.

Now three years have passed already—though it seems like it was only yesterday when we first got married. I wondered what forty-seven years of marriage could have been like for my parents! I've always felt *really* loved, protected and cared for by Bob, and am truly amazed at what a good friend he's turned out to be…'course, I joke now that it's always good to have a handyman around too, instead of always having to fix everything myself!

A few weeks after our third anniversary, Bob, mom and I, and our three cats made our move to Bingham, Maine. Life here, in a fine old Victorian with a furnace that works like a charm…so far…is quite different from Staten Island! Here in Bingham, hardly anyone locks their front doors at night, and most people don't even lock their cars, something that mom can't believe.

We gave mom a good-sized room on the first floor so she doesn't have to navigate any stairs. Bob and I have our bedroom upstairs with an enclosed porch overlooking the back half acre. In the warmer weather, we'll be able to sleep out on the porch (or even the back half acre!) if we want.

Mom loves to help out in the kitchen all the time, and she's adjusting beautifully to her new home, no small feat for someone her age. She loves Bob like a son. And I am ecstatic every day not to have to commute to a corporate position in a big city. I simply walk down the hall, into my office, and start my workday.

There are a couple of things we miss from New York, though…great Italian food and Italian pastry—but there's one thing I believe will always remain the same: mom still locks the front door at night!

ABOUT THE AUTHOR: Barbara Dunne considers herself a late bloomer. Well into her fabulous fifties, she welcomed downsizing as an opportunity to become a successful entrepreneur. After a 30 year executive assistant career in corporate America, Barbara now partners virtually with small business owners, coaches, authors, and other entrepreneurs to free them from the burden of administrative tasks. Overwhelmed busy professionals *can* find balance between their business and personal lives, and partnering with a virtual assistant *is* the solution! Barbara recently relocated from New York City to the beautiful sleepy little town of Bingham, Maine with her husband, mom, and three cats.

Barbara Molnar Dunne
www.barbaradunne.com
barbara@barbaradunne.com
207-672-3119

Living from the Heart
Kathy Fyler

I raced into the driveway, pulled the car to a quick stop, sprinted to the front door, and charged into the house. When I saw my parents, I burst into tears and sobbed, "I have to have open heart surgery!"

I remember the startled look on my mom's face as she hugged me. I could almost hear the thoughts going through her head. "She's only twenty-six...she's healthy and active...she only has a little bit of a murmur...how can this be happening; what's this all about?"

My dad wanted to know the facts and *all* of the details. But at this point, I didn't even know them. As a nurse, I thought I knew a lot, but standing on the other end of a health issue was new territory for me. They wanted to run more tests right away to see how quickly they needed to perform surgery, and how extensive it might be. Usually calm and not easily rattled, this news shook me to my core.

I spent the next several weeks undergoing tests and studying more about the surgery. There was a hole in my heart between my two atriums, and apparently a vein from my lung was incorrectly routed to my heart. Because I'd had this condition since birth, if they didn't fix it now, my lungs would be permanently damaged and I'd suffer heart disease down the road. I scheduled the surgery for July—only two months away!

The doctors called this kind of open heart surgery "routine" and said that, since I was young and healthy, I should recover quickly. *Routine?* It wasn't routine to me! I thought that when they saw through your chest, pull your ribs apart, and manipulate your heart, it's referred to as *major* surgery!

Fear began to creep in, and I started to imagine all sorts of horrible "what if" scenarios...what if I died during surgery? What if they found something else when they were in there? What if there were complications and I became a vegetable? What about the scar that would run down the middle of my chest? Being a nurse, I had seen patients with scars that looked like huge, ugly zippers, those paralyzed due to a stroke, and some who had to remain on medications for the rest of their lives. And I was only twenty-six!

Thank goodness for my mom. We spent a lot of time together that May and June. We didn't talk much about the pending operation; instead we treated ourselves to things that we wouldn't normally, were it not for the upcoming surgery. Instead of playing golf a couple of times a month, we played twice a week. We rented a golf cart instead of walking. We lunched, laughed and enjoyed each other's company. It seemed that skipping the Friday house cleaning now and then, and spending an extra ten dollars on lunch no longer seemed to matter that much.

Under the Knife

The day before the surgery, I arrived at the hospital with my parents, and if it weren't for the pesky pre-op procedures, I'd say it was actually quite an enjoyable day. Many co-workers and friends visited me throughout the day, and it flew by quickly.

I remember walking to the elevator with my father as he left for home that evening. He hugged me and said "I love you." Growing up in my family, there was plenty of love, but not too many verbal and physical demonstrations of it. His words and gestures comforted me that night, but still the pending surgery seemed ominous and I was frightened.

I walked back to my room wondering if my dad and I were thinking the same thing. Did we really *know* each other? I knew him as my father, the man who worked long, hard hours to take really good care of us, the guy who loved family activities, the father who was always there when we needed him...and yet, it felt like we'd just started to get to know each other. I yearned for a deeper connection. I prayed that my time wouldn't be cut short, and that we'd get that chance.

The nurse woke me up at six a.m. the next morning to administer a valium so I could relax. Great, I thought, now I had an extra hour to worry…

At seven a.m., the stretcher arrived. Two orderlies dressed in white wheeled me down a long corridor into a big, cold, sterile room. I still remember their silence and robot-like movements.   As I lay on the stretcher under the glare of what felt like a huge spotlight, I thought to myself: this is not the kind of spotlight I really want to be in!

It was surreal, lonely and scary. So this is it, I thought; hopefully, it will be over soon. The anesthesiologist gave me some medication and told me to count backwards from one hundred…ninety-nine…ninety-eight…

The next couple of days whizzed by in a blur—probably a blessing. At one point, I woke up to the pain and fogginess of post-surgery, and a wave of gratitude surged through me. The worst was over. I'd made it through the surgery. I was alive…

I recall countless doctors, nurses, respiratory therapists, aids and family passing through my room. They removed my breathing tube and sat me up. Soon, fewer and fewer staff came in and out—all good signs for my recovery.

Yet I began to sense that something was not right.   I felt overwhelmingly exhausted and struggled to get enough air. Though doped up from the pain medications and not fully conscious, somehow I managed to convey this to my dad, who immediately called the cardiologist. To this day, I don't remember actually having had this conversation with my father, but I'm grateful I was somehow able to communicate and he listened.

In what seemed like an instant *and* an eternity, doctors and nurses surrounded my bed. I remember them telling me "your lungs are filing with fluid and you're not getting enough oxygen. We have to put the breathing tube back in."

At that point, I began to separate from my body. As I floated to the upper corner of the room and watched from above, I saw below me the intensely frenetic energy of the doctors and nurses who worked on me. In emergency mode, there was movement and panic; up above, I felt only peace and calm.

Suddenly I heard the words "You have to hang in—don't give up!"

The next moment I re-entered my body and felt myself lying on the bed. The breathing machine made a noise and I could feel the oxygen rush into my lungs. Ahhh...it was as if I'd been drowning, and suddenly my head surfaced above the water. The struggle over, my tired body slipped into a deep sleep.

The next day I woke up to see an oncologist smiling down at me. OH MY GOD, I thought, I have cancer! Luckily for me he was also a hematologist and that's why he was there to see me. He explained that there'd been a problem with my blood during my first surgery.

"My *first* surgery?" He explained to me that two days before, immediately after my initial surgery, I'd actually been taken back into the operating room where they opened my chest a second time because I was "bleeding out" in the recovery room. It turned out I possess a rare blood cell shape, which caused my red blood cells to split open as they passed through the heart-lung machine.

Thank God my cousin Marcia—a nurse at the hospital—remembered I had some type of anemia and told the doctors. If they hadn't figured out what caused the bleeding I might never have survived. Wow, two very close calls with death in two days!

Epilogue

As I near my fiftieth birthday and reflect back, I realize now what I didn't then. I had come away from this experience with a new sense of confidence and purpose.

I decided to go back to school and work towards a graduate degree. I chose to change my nursing specialty to the Open Heart ICU. Here I experienced a great deal of compassion and a connection with patients and families that I didn't have before my own surgery. I ended a toxic long-term relationship, and opened myself up to new experiences, new friends, and true love.

Over the next few years, I changed careers, started a business, and moved from the state in which I'd lived my entire life. I felt free and ready for pretty much anything. I now have the close relationship I longed for with my dad. We both say "I love you" easily and often.

If I hadn't cheated death twice, I don't know if I'd be as grateful for my life now. While my appreciation of the fragility and uncertainty of my time here on earth has grown exponentially, so has my desire to connect with others.

Today I incorporate into my life and soul the message I received from watching myself as I floated above in the corner of the room that day: I am not meant to be a spectator; I am meant to be the creator of my own life! My work with our networking company, Powerful You!, reinforces for me daily the importance of human connection, and my desire to open myself to life and love.

Through the years, I've often heard the words "you have to hang in— don't give up," and they have served me well. Now, fully open, I look back and realize that was the year I began to live from my heart.

ABOUT THE AUTHOR: Kathy Fyler's diverse career includes being a Nurse in Oncology, AIDS and Cardiac Units, a Project Manager for a technology firm, and owner of a $5 million sign and display company. Kathy felt an urge to make "more of a contribution to what matters most in this world". Using her experience and passion for technology and people, in 2005 she co-founded Powerful You! Women's Network to fulfill her mission of assisting women in creating connections via the internet, and in face-to-face meetings and events. Kathy loves to travel the country connecting with the inspiring women of Powerful You!

Kathy Fyler
Powerful You! Women's Network
www.powerfulyou.com
kathy.fyler@powerfulyou.com
973-248-1262

Second Chance at Life and Love

Jill Garaffa

"Will You Marry Me?" Ari asked as we waited for his plane to depart. The whole thing was surreal; a scene out of a movie, or someone else's life. I stared at the ring in disbelief.

It was the question I thought would never come. Still single and auditioning potential husbands for the past two decades, I'd resigned myself to the belief that, clearly, there must be something wrong with me. For years, I was haunted by images of my future self as a grouchy old house frau who wears a bathrobe, and lives in a house filled with cats.

Most amazing was the fact that this gorgeous, blue-eyed man kneeling before me, ring in hand, was my first love from high school: The one that got away; the one I never forgot.

The touch stone to which all other men were unconsciously and unfairly compared, Ari's proposal confirmed that my dating life had finally come full circle. We'd re-connected on Facebook a year prior to this moment, only a few months after I'd celebrated my twenty-first anniversary of recovery from bulimia.

Soon after reconnecting and still reeling from the miracle of it all, I traveled up to my attic to dig out the dusty box containing my old journals from high school. It was as if I'd entered a time machine. My eyes danced across the pages and memories of the night we'd met, our first date, our first kiss, the prom, and how we'd met each other's parents, all came back to life.

Memories of the beach, our friends, parties and concerts shined through like photographs, highlighting our great times together, particularly the moments we knew it was love. Our connection was timeless. We were best friends, "soul-mates" we declared.

While blessed with a truly amazing connection, the pictures of us nonetheless carried with them an ugly reminder of the turmoil that raged inside of me at that time. Forgotten memories, buried long ago, resurfaced, and I found it hard to believe the person I was reading about now was actually me.

The entire time we dated in high school I was held hostage by an eating disorder. It had been a source of pain for us both. I remember the look of concern and helplessness on his face at times as he watched me struggle.

It all started when I turned twelve. A year punctuated with so many "firsts"—period, bra, boyfriend, kiss—it also marked a great deal of pain and loss for me. My best friend's mom succumbed to cancer and, a year later, her dad took his own life. My older brother wasn't around as much anymore…he'd fallen in love with the woman he eventually married. My middle brother left to join the Navy, and I lost several friends as our changing interests caused us to grow apart.

I started overeating because eating made me feel better. I didn't know I was eating to cope with anxiety, I just knew that I gained weight like it was my job.

I remember feeling uncomfortable because my clothes no longer fit the same way. But I didn't feel self-conscious until my father, in his misguided but loving parental attempt to shield me from the pain of any future rejection, uttered his infamous words: "If you're fat, you will never have a boyfriend…boys don't like fat girls. You need to lose weight!"

His words stung like acid. I didn't know I was fat! My dad said it, not once, but many times. He fought with my mother and blamed her because I was getting "chubby". It was apparently a big deal. I felt like a disappointment. This led to another twelfth year "first"—my first diet.

Not long after my declaration to diet, as we sat in science class, our teacher dimmed the lights and started a movie projector. What unfolded was a story about a girl with bulimia. I sat at my desk, enthralled. I had never heard of this condition. Make yourself throw up? As I watched the movie, which was intended to scare us, my wheels began to turn. "That's brilliant." I thought. "What a great idea. I can eat anything I want and not gain weight!"

And, so it began. I went home that day after school, and vividly remember eating a yogurt and deliberately making myself throw up just to see if I could do it. Victorious, I declared this my new strategy. My life changed that day.

Throughout the next several years, binging and purging grew from occasional escape to regular habit. I'd steal, sneak and hide food, all the while lying to my parents and making up stories about the missing food in the house. When I got my driver's license and a job, things got even worse. I had money and complete freedom, and my "secret life" spiraled out of control.

I'd eat entire pizzas, dozens of donuts, and gallons of ice cream in one sitting. By the time I went away to college, I binged and purged an average of five times per day. It was no longer a habit—it was a lifestyle. The act itself became addictive. I was obsessed. I spent hours every day and hundreds of dollars every month on binging and purging.

Out of the Frying Pan, Into the Fire...

Despite the chaos in my mind, my outward life appeared quite normal. My grades were excellent, and I had an active social life, filled with friends and activities. Yet I spent every day addicted to this disgusting habit—I couldn't stop. While I knew intellectually that I had a serious problem, my combined sense of apathy, guilt and humiliation allowed no willingness on my part to do anything about it.

My hair started to fall out; my skin was dry and flaky. Always exhausted, I had dark circles under my eyes, constant mouth sores, and was often uncomfortably bloated. If anyone asked, I was always "fine." I later learned that "fine" is an acronym for "f'd up, insecure, neurotic and emotional."

I started to throw up blood. My heartbeat became irregular and I had dizzy spells. I was only nineteen, but felt like I was ninety-nine. I developed a real fear of dying. I fantasized that my parents or college roommates would find me dead, slumped over the toilet bowl. The thought of hurting them broke my heart. That just wasn't how I wanted to go.

Eventually, something deep inside of me shifted. I was faced with my own truth: I was an addict. Addicted to food like other people are addicted to drugs. I really wanted to get better but I couldn't stop. I knew I would die if I didn't make some serious changes. I also knew I couldn't do it alone.

I sat on a bench at the beach and watched the seagulls and the sun set, and breathed in the sound of the waves. It was a moment of peace; just me and God there on the beach.

I prayed hard for help and a sense of calm came over me. I knew, with absolute certainty and clarity that I was done with this way of life. I promised God that, if he let me live and get through this, I would make something of myself.

Two days later I entered a treatment facility. I began to untangle the mess of dysfunctional and distorted thoughts that had taken over my mind. I realized I wasn't alone. I learned how to live without using food or other substances. I learned that pain is our greatest teacher, and that to numb it only prolongs it.

After leaving the treatment center, I became very active in twelve-step recovery programs. For many years, I not only attended meetings, I led them as well. In addition, I sponsored women, performed service, celebrated anniversaries, and attended conventions.

One day, many years later, I met a woman at a party who called herself a "life coach." I'd never heard of such a thing at that time. She offered me a complimentary session and I became fascinated.

While my recovery program was working well, other areas of my life needed a tune up. I still struggled with clutter, finances and time management—I was constantly busy and overcommitted. Though in constant motion, there was no movement forward, and no balance. I immediately hired her.

After six months of weekly conversations with this woman, my life took a 180 degree turn. So impressed with the outcome, I decided to get certified and become a life coach myself. Now involved in the world of coaching for more than seven years, I am humbled and grateful at how far I've come, and *who* I've become.

Through the experience of coaching I managed to get to the core of what was going on. I investigated my view of the world, my beliefs and my values, and confronted my fears. I uncovered what I like to call "blind spots" in how I was relating to the world, with both food and life in general. I felt calm yet powerful, and I began to take action in all the areas of my life that mattered to me. I was empowered.

Epilogue

Ari and I parted ways at the age of nineteen when both of us agreed that we would embrace the opportunity to go away to college and fully experience life. We each journeyed into the world, lived our separate lives and eventually lost touch with each other. Then, one day, God brought us back together again, better and stronger than when we were teenagers.

The woman I grew to be bears little resemblance to the insecure teenager I'd been when we first dated. Today I own my beauty and my power. Clear about who I am, I possess a confidence and wisdom that wasn't present before.

After a twenty-four year separation, here was Ari, on bended knee, ring in hand, proposing marriage a year after our first date. The ending— and beginning!—of our story. With the confidence and enthusiasm of absolute certainty, I looked into his gorgeous blue eyes, smiled, and replied, "Yes, absolutely yes—I will marry you!"

ABOUT THE AUTHOR: A certified professional coach specializing in health & wellness, Jill holds a B.S. in Occupational Therapy from Kean University, and formal training program certificates in life coaching from both Comprehensive Coaching U and The Institute for Professional Excellence in Coaching. Jill's career as an occupational therapist reached a turning point in 2002 when she transformed her passion for health into a full time coaching business to help prevent the kinds of conditions she'd treated as a therapist. Jill is the owner and founder of Seeds of Change Health & Wellness Coaching, which provides lifestyle coaching services to individuals and groups, from families to corporations.

Jill Garaffa, OTR/L, CPC
Seeds of Change Health & Wellness Coaching
www.seedsofchangecoaching.com
jill@seedsofchangecoaching.com ~ 732-859-6962

Straight from the Heart
AmondaRose Igoe

My father disappeared when I was six years old and I didn't see him again until he lay in a casket at the funeral parlor when I was ten. How could I have known that the father and daughter reunion I'd dreamt about would take place at my father's funeral? I never knew for sure why he chose to just vanish and never contact us again.

Up until the age of six, my life was what most would call very normal. I lived in a middle class neighborhood in a two story house and a big backyard with my mom, dad, older brother, and our rambunctious puppy Jolie, an English setter, who looked a lot like a black and white Dalmatian. Just like most families in the 1960's, dad went to work every day and mom stayed home to take care of the kids.

My life turned upside down one day when I arrived home from kindergarten and noticed my dad's green car was in front of the house. This seemed strange to me because my dad was usually at work when I came home from school. When I realized his car had been in the same spot for two days and I hadn't seen him the whole time, I became overwhelmed with the feeling that something was seriously wrong.

I ran into the house as fast as my little six year old legs could carry me. I had to find my mom. If anyone would know where daddy was, certainly she'd be the one. I burst through the front door and screamed "Mom! Mom! Where's Dad? Where's Dad?" I knew something wasn't right.

My mother looked at me with her sad eyes and said "I don't know."

"Are you looking for him, mom? Are you looking for daddy?" I implored. She told me she had the police looking for him, but no one knew where he was. It was as if my father literally vanished into thin air!

Months passed, and my mother did everything humanly possible to find my father, including hiring a detective. No one knew what had happened to him, even my dad's parents. He literally *had* disappeared without a clue.

I cried myself to sleep at night. I prayed over and over again in my bedroom to God, asking him to please bring my dad back home again. As each year passed, I began to give up hope that I'd ever see my father again.

My mother soldiered on, picked up the pieces of her broken life, and rose to the occasion. She worked until she was emotionally drained and physically exhausted to keep a roof over our heads and food in our mouths. An amazingly strong woman, I realized she could have chosen to just leave like my dad, but she didn't.

But signs of strain existed. One day when I was eight, I returned home from school to find my puppy Jolie missing. Devastated, I asked my mom where she could be. She told me that the dog was just too much trouble and that she'd had to give her away. I was devastated. Angry that Jolie was gone—and that she'd been given away while I was at school—I was hurt that I didn't even have a chance to say goodbye.

By the time I was ten there'd been no news at all about my father. Then one day my grandmother, my father's mother, called to say she'd read an article in the New York Times newspaper about a man who died in a fire. The man's last name was the same as ours, the same name as my father and my grandparents. When she recognized her own unusual last name of Igoe, she discovered her son had been hiding out in New York City and that he'd lost his life in a fire.

I used to say that he'd left because "daddy needed to do what daddy needed to do." I don't know why. Perhaps, in my young mind, I felt it necessary to defend my father for his irresponsible actions, even though he'd hurt me so. Maybe somewhere deep inside my mind, I knew it was the best thing for everyone.

A Ray of Light

After that, my family's life changed forever. My father's disappearance and death left a hole in my heart. However, in my deepest and darkest hour I was sent a ray of light in the form of my very special angel—my mother's oldest brother Uncle Dominic.

Uncle Dom—a quiet and beautiful soul—showed me unconditional love, unlike my own father. Not one to use big expressive words, he actually didn't say much at all. But I knew without a shadow of a doubt that he loved me to my core. He changed the course of my life forever.

My own father had told me he loved me; however it was my Uncle Dom who *showed* me he loved me. From him I learned what it means to really take care of the people you love. Every Sunday, rain or shine, he would drive an hour each way to spend time with our family. Talk about love and commitment; he was always there for us. Part of me was convinced that he drove to our house every Sunday to be there for me and to make sure I was okay.

My Uncle Dom's love was simple and pure, and he expressed how much he cared in extraordinary and unique ways. He called me "Pachaba Bird," a special silly name he created just for me. Even today it reminds me of our special connection.

When I was with him, it didn't matter what we were doing. We'd spend hours tending the backyard garden, and in the summer he'd take our family to the amusement park. I remember one day he spent every cent he had so that he could win a huge four foot pink teddy bear. He wanted to surprise me with it. I knew then, without a shadow a doubt, there wasn't anything he wouldn't have done for me.

Then one day, he suddenly became critically ill. I remember racing to the hospital because all the major organs in his body had started to shut down. No one saw it coming. I'll never forget the day when he told me "Pachaba Bird, I don't' think I am going to make it."

I wanted to tell him that he would be okay, but I couldn't speak through my tears. How would I manage life without him? Panic-stricken, stressed and anxious, I thought to myself "no! I love you—you can't leave me too! I need you here with me!" Within a few days my beloved Uncle Dom was gone.

His funeral, filled with so many people who shared stories of how he'd helped them, illustrated that everyone loved him as much as I did because his heart was open wide. He never asked for anything in return. If someone needed a hand, my Uncle Dom was right there to help them. It became clear that day that he'd been a gift to each person with whom he'd come in contact.

When challenges and significant personal obstacles crossed my path, I had my Uncle Dom's love to see me through. Today, I believe he is an angel guiding me from above. So strongly do I feel his presence around me that I even believe he helped orchestrate the day I met my wonderful and loving husband Tony, more than twenty years ago.

We all need someone who believes in us, even when we don't believe in ourselves. He kept his heart open wide and showed others the power of unconditional love, and in doing so allowed me to learn to do the same. Through his love, I know that living and loving from the heart is the greatest gift *I* can give another. That was Uncle Dom's legacy; his greatest gift to me.

I *used* to believe I was a victim of life's circumstances. I thought that others should feel sorry for me because of the negative things that happened in my life. At one point, I could have cornered the market on the "poor, poor, pitiful me syndrome."

Conquering this syndrome, however, has allowed this formerly shy, scared, and broken little girl to evolve into a woman with confidence, power and passion. I walked through my fears and released the past that bound me. Today, I show others how their painful past experiences can truly be a gift when utilized to connect emotionally with others.

An example of how *anyone* can triumph over tragedy, I am committed to touching the lives of millions in a positive way in this lifetime. I now show up in this world in a changed way, touched by the love of my angel Uncle Dom.

Through his never-ending and truly unconditional love, he showed me that, although my father had chosen to leave, I still had fatherly love to guide me. He left a glowing and permanent impression on my heart. In honor of him, I plan to spend the rest of my life speaking, living, and loving—straight from the heart.

ABOUT THE AUTHOR: AmondaRose Igoe is the is the author of Pain-Free Public Speaking, a contributing author in the #1 Best Selling book series "Chicken Soup for the Soul" and was interviewed on the FOX 4 Television Station. As a Leading Expert in Public Speaking, she has a unique ability to help others connect with the mind, heart and spirit of their audiences which makes her a highly sought after speaker and trainer. She ignites the atmosphere with her empowering message, contagious enthusiasm and real results. When looking for a Professional Speaker and Trainer who specializes in public speaking, look no further than AmondaRose.

AmondaRose Igoe
High Performance Speaking Training and Consulting
www.HighPerformanceSpeaking.com
561-498-8919

The Me In Me

Audrey Keip

When I walked into my doctor's office that day, it was with the hope that he'd be kind enough to provide me with a note for a leave of absence from work for two weeks. What I heard instead shocked me.

"Audrey, I can see you've hit bottom and that you're depressed," my doctor began. "I'm going to recommend that you start on some medication and take a minimum of three months off. I'm worried that if you don't, you're headed for a stroke or a heart attack. At the least, we need to get you out of this depressed state."

My face turned beet red, tears welled up in my eyes and I felt one or two dropping down the sides of my cheeks.

Me depressed? Me, the happy-go-lucky one? The one who never bothers anyone with her problems? What is he talking about? I just came here to get a note for some well deserved time off!

The doctor was still talking as my mind drifted in and out, thinking about all that's happened, and was happening in my life. I walked past the nurse on my way out, said bye to the secretary, but I was in a daze.

I felt light headed, and I couldn't wait to get outside for some fresh air. But that was not unusual for me, as the doctor's office was never my favorite place. I must have sat in my car for ten minutes before I realized I had a prescription in my hand. My mind continued to race in every direction—past, present and future.

On my way to the drug store, my mind retraced all that had happened to me these past six months. I walked slowly and nervously, prescription in hand, out of the drug store. I remember the cool March breeze and falling snow flakes as they landed on my still heated cheeks.

Once home I sat there not really believing what had just happened to me. I looked at the pill bottle still in my hand my whole body began to shake. Suddenly and without warning I burst into a seemingly unstoppable flood of tears.

Life throws us curves, and sometimes in an instant, things can change. But thinking back now I see it really was a process—I just never saw it coming. Six months earlier I'd left my children's father. We'd drifted so far from each other that communication literally ceased; we became two separate individuals living under one roof.

This not only upset my children, it didn't sit well with my family either, particularly my father. Catholic and very strict in his religion, my father had raised nine children on a large farm. His heart and soul were in the land of farming. In fact, he was far happier to train us as farmers then to think about any of us pursuing an education.

I dreamed of being a teacher. I was the third youngest and, although never exactly poor, when I approached my father for money for school, he told me I was on my own. So I borrowed money from my brother and attended the college for business and clerical bookkeeping. But, forced to stop to work for a few years in order to support myself, I never went back.

The Blame Game

It's so easy to blame others—if only my father had agreed to pay for school—but in the end I realized it was really my choice to quit. I settled for work in an accounting firm. After several years, I started getting bored and restless. I took some night classes to upgrade my work, but my life simply wasn't moving forward.

When upper management changed at work, so did my job. Change appeared to be coming at lightning speed and I couldn't keep up. Lost, both my professional and personal world seemed to unravel around me.

I left the bottle of pills sitting on the cupboard where I could see them every day. I knew I'd never take even one, but seeing them reminded me what my body and my higher self were trying to telling me—I needed time off to concentrate on *me*.

So many mornings I woke up with my eyes pasted shut from crying the night before. By this time everyone knew—my children, co-workers and family—I needed three months off to recuperate. I felt like a mess and a disappointment, alone and broken in a world full of people but at the same time totally empty inside.

My family disapproved of me—some did not communicate with me at all. I came to realize that they judged me from the outside; they couldn't see the bruises on the inside. My father expressed disappointment, but deep down inside I believe he approved in his own way. I'd always tried to please him and make him feel proud of me. I knew his strictness was his way of wanting the best for us all.

I realized that if I hadn't hit bottom I'd never have slowed down my body and mind enough to stop and listen to my inner voice. In an odd kind of way, my sense that my father really did approve confirmed for me that I had a higher spirit on my side.

My slowly blossoming spiritual awareness became an essential means of guidance on a daily basis. I'd always lived within my comfort zone, and I still struggle with that to this day. I've never put myself first so learning to do so was like entering uncharted waters. But I knew the time had come and that it was necessary for my survival.

Regardless of what other people thought, I knew in my heart I needed to take steps in order to keep my life moving forward. Right or wrong, I discovered a spirit within that finally came to life. With the help of Lois, a wonderful person who came into my life just at that moment when I needed her most, I discovered that life is a series of lessons.

She taught me that no one can *force* me to change, that change is up to me. I had to be willing to go within, to truly *want* to make changes; it had nothing to do with anyone else. I learned that I had to allow my friends and family to be who they are, and to just love them.

And I had to deal with the "real" me—but who was that? I blamed myself for all that was happening, but slowly began to understand that my way of thinking had nothing to do with the real me, it only blocked me from seeing the good within.

The stress I experienced was self-created! I suddenly realized how I used stress as an excuse to protect myself from my fear of change, and how I then could rationalize not taking any responsibility for my own emotions. And this kept me from moving forward to achieve inner harmony and peace. I soon found out that it's impossible to experience stress/fear and love at the same time. So why not choose the more positive one?

I began to look at life with new eyes. The world around me had always been there, but now I began to experience it through the eyes of a child, the eyes of wonder. I felt connected on a higher level, and am grateful for every single day.

I may have hit bottom but I needed to go deep within to discover that the true me was so very much alive and well. Challenges arrived when I was ready to meet them head on in order to grow and learn. My true spirit alive, I no longer hide behind my fears, and am now truly the happy-go-lucky person that I only pretended to be in the past.

Those few months of forced time off became my salvation. I used the time to study financial planning, and researched a more opportune place to work where they would train me and allow me to finish my studies in the financial field. My passion became educating clients to understand their finances, because building a solid financial future enables us all to achieve future growth, as it nurtures our emotional and physical selves.

I believe that abundance and prosperity is about allowing ourselves to accept. Each of us has the power within to realize our fondest dreams. I've learned that, when we don't get what we want, on some level we are not willing to receive.

As the months and years have passed I found that my dreams are within my reach. My job *is* as a teacher, perhaps not as I'd originally imagined, but in an even better way. Once I let go of the past and the worries about the future, I found a *me* inside of me that I'd never known existed.

ABOUT THE AUTHOR: Licensed financial and insurance advisor and educator Audrey Keip takes a holistic approach to helping you plan your life and fulfill your dreams. Committed to providing her clients with superior solutions at every stage of life, Audrey believes dreams *can* become reality! But she knows every dream needs a plan! Let *Keip*

Financial Services assist you to devise the plan to achieve those dreams and enjoy peace of mind. Your *dreams* are her *goals*, and Audrey's mission is to manifest your success in the best ways possible. Her success comes from helping *you* succeed!

Audrey Keip
Keip Financial Services
519-364-7526

Wedding Bell Blues
Monica Leggett

"Here I am, over 30 years old, on my own for several years now, and I feel like a scared little kid again." I sat at my desk, as Olga poured out her heart to me via Skype. "My mom wants one thing, my fiancé wants another, and I'm stuck in the middle. I don't know how I am going to make my mom see that I want a small, modern celebration, not the traditional wedding she and my dad are expecting.

I love my Mom, but I feel like she wants to control everything."

Olga's scenario sounded all too familiar to me. I'd trained to become a relationship coach—and chose to work with brides and their moms—precisely because I'd experienced many of the same issues with which Olga was now dealing.

Except in my case, *I* had been the mom who wouldn't let go of her expectations. I had to learn how to stop being "MOM in charge" and accept and engage with my child as an adult.

A few years earlier, my middle child and only son Russ became the first of my three children to get engaged. He and his fiancé began planning a small wedding. They had already bought a house, planned a family, and the wedding was the final step to celebrate their commitment to each other.

New at being the parent of a groom to be, Russ and I fought over the guest list. Though I didn't realize it at the time, our disagreement had less to do with the number of people at his wedding than with our different expectations, lack of proper boundaries, and my attempt to impose my own agenda.

The apple hadn't fallen far from the tree; we were two very stubborn people who didn't know how to relate to each other. He and his fiancée were determined to keep their wedding small. My definition of small, when it comes to our family weddings, is about one hundred people. Their goal was forty. Unfortunately our definition of the word "small" varied greatly!

I'm the seventh of ten kids, and our immediate family alone is more than forty people—and that doesn't even include extended relatives and close friends whom I'd always pictured present at my children's weddings.

Fearful that we'd lose face in front of all the relatives—who'd known for a year about the wedding—I defended my position and my pride at the expense of our relationship.

"How can we invite some and not others?" I asked him. "You can't do that!" I didn't consciously intend to hurt my son or his fiancée, but the ensuing struggle of "I'm right and you're wrong" injured our relationship in the end.

We ended up with a compromise, and though the wedding turned out beautifully, with twenty-eight family members in attendance, I knew it was time to redesign our parent/child relationship to reflect the new dynamics of adulthood. I just hadn't discovered how…yet.

The Times They are a Changin'

When my older sister, a renowned relationship and leadership coach, talked me into attending a weekend life coach training class, I was a respiratory therapist, working crazy hours in a hospital ICU. I wanted more flexibility and a calmer environment, but one in which I could still make a difference in people's lives.

That weekend was like none I'd ever experienced. For two magical days I found myself surrounded by curious and energizing people. I learned about perspectives, goals, and thinking outside the box.

This experience opened the door to my awakening. It took eighteen intense months to complete the training and certification to be a life coach—and it was all worth it. I lapped up every new concept and applied it to my life as a wife, mother and business owner.

Byron Katie's book "Loving What Is" also proved to be an important and insightful tool in my continued growth. This work shifted my whole perspective about finding fault with others and trying to influence them to see it my way. No more "he should do this" or "she should have done that" for me!

I finally understood that I only have control over MYSELF, no one else. No matter how much I want someone to do a certain thing or think a certain way, it's beyond my control. I discovered that to believe otherwise only made me more anxious or angry.

I knew there was so much more to learn about relationships and I was hungry to understand the concepts and tools that I could use in my own life, as well as for my clients. I'd learned that relationships between two or more people are not just a dialogue; they are a separate living and breathing entity between people. In order for individuals to feel safe, heard and supported, their relationship needs to be strong and open and nurtured with conscious positive intention.

So I followed my life coach certification with five long weekends of relationship training, filled with experiential coursework aimed at understanding relationship systems. I used my struggle with letting go as inspiration, and channeled my energies into learning how to teach others to empower their relationships.

I came to understand and identify the "toxins" that weakened my own relationships: defensiveness and judgment, to name two. I explored the antidotes to these toxins in order to find a way to strengthen my relationships through forgiveness, open-mindedness, and the willingness to be influenced. I also learned to identify my "hidden self," the one that got triggered whenever I felt threatened, the one that exhibited negative behavior that I would later regret.

As I related this new information to my own life, I realized how I'd approached my family relationships in a defensive manner. In the case of my son's wedding, I'd retreated into my own corner, and he into his, and we fought for our own agendas.

I realized that my worst offense was that I defended my position and my pride at the expense of our relationship. Through my training I began to understand how we could have laid out a joint vision, and by working towards this vision, strengthened our relationship instead of damaging it. I resolved to go forward with stronger relationships as my goal.

I immediately put my theories to the test with my children and husband. I began to express my thoughts and feelings proactively, and found they followed suit. We then "designed" our new roles, and talked about how we could support each other, and how we'd act with each other during conflicts. We openly shared in a way we hadn't before. Everything is out in the open now.

Many family relationships end because one last slight breaks the camel's back. Parents in particular find it difficult to turn off parental *power* and transition to an *empowered* adult relationship. Now I focus my attention as a coach on teaching others how to *prevent* those slights. I have learned to accomplish this through the facilitation of powerful and proactive discussions that design ground rules and set a common vision.

Goin' to the Chapel

"Mom, Chris and I are engaged!" my daughter Melissa informed her father and me. It had been over two years since my son's wedding and I reminded myself that this time it would be different. *Now* I was prepared. *Now* I applied all of my training to the process of wedding planning.

First, we designed our "partnership" and worked as a team. In doing so, we eliminated all the drama that typically accompanies such a stressful life transition. There were no fights about guest lists or wedding vendors, budgets or décor.

Melissa's sister Christine was a key member of the team and we clearly defined our roles and expectations. We did everything on time, within budget, and the way the bride and groom wanted. Melissa's wedding proved to me that family members can work together in harmony toward a clear vision.

I now know that I have transformed from a woman living unconsciously in her relationships to someone who makes powerful choices to protect and nurture them. I understand that it's up to me to bring a positive atmosphere to a relationship. I'm now able to listen with an open mind and an open heart, and take steps to protect and strengthen my existing relationships.

Criticism, contempt and blame have no place in a healthy relationship. Acknowledgment, appreciation, and acceptance, not to mention an occasional apology, can make all the difference in the world.

I immediately identified Olga's anxiety as she related her list of concerns about her mother trying to "control" her wedding. During the three short months we worked together, Olga learned how to speak up for herself, set joint boundaries and expectations with her parents, and plan her new life with her husband.

Olga told me she felt closer now to her parents than ever before, and was jubilant when she reported to me that her mom had told her "I just want you to be happy." The final wedding plan contained a few compromises from both sides, but it ultimately turned into the wedding that Olga and her husband very much wanted—a memorable celebration from which to launch their new life together.

On the day of her wedding, Olga was so relaxed and happy that her hairdresser was sure she could not be getting married that day. "I've never seen a bride so calm!" she exclaimed. It's amazing what peace of mind and strong relationships can do for your confidence!

I feel triumphant when a bride tells me she's gained a new respect and appreciation for her mother, or that she's been able to express her goals and dreams clearly to her fiancé.

Now hard at work writing a book for brides, I've also begun a blog that shares my tools, tips and strategies for improved and empowered relationships during the wedding planning process.

My goal? To help as many as possible avoid becoming victims of this stressful life transition, and to create more empowered and happy brides like Olga and my daughter—not to mention happy moms!

ABOUT THE AUTHOR: Monica Leggett is a certified life and relationship coach. She works with people all over the US and Canada, empowering them through life transformations such as career changes, empty nest syndrome, and marriage transitions. Also a wedding coach, Monica helps brides, couples and moms successfully negotiate through this often-stressful transition, teaching them to build stronger relationships along the way. Monica and her husband Steve have been married thirty years, experienced the weddings of all three of their children and are expecting their third grandchild soon. Monica is an author, presenter, volunteer, and group facilitator in CT.

Monica Leggett
www.NewStepsLifeCoaching.com
www.TheEmpoweredBride.com
Monica@newstepslifecoaching.com
203-209-5462

Winning the Weight Game
Michelle Marin

I stood in the kitchen, alone. Without any forethought, I grabbed the tantalizing loaf of fresh bread I'd bought earlier in the day, tore off hunks, and ate them as if I was starving.

Okay, enough is enough, I thought, so I went back to my book in the living room. Twenty minutes later I was back in the kitchen again mangling the loaf of bread.

I compulsively rummaged through the cabinets for anything else that might strike my fancy. I hurriedly twisted the top off a jar of peanut butter and spread it generously on the bread. I washed it down with some soda and a handful of mixed nuts. My belly was aching, but I couldn't get the food in fast enough. When will this end, I asked myself. The voice of reason sent me back to the couch for a while, but soon enough I was back to the bread. Before I knew it, the entire loaf was gone.

Finally, I lay on the coach, numb from my frenzied eating fest, and fell asleep. The next morning would inevitably bring a food hangover, and incredible guilt and shame for my lack of control.

For as long as I can remember, I've been a "foodie." I used food to celebrate, to numb my feelings, to entertain myself, or just for immediate gratification. While intellectually I understood that we were all brought into this world with the innate drive to eat when we're hungry and stop when we're satisfied, somewhere along the line I lost the ability to feed myself appropriately.

I lost touch with the concept that food is fuel. During my strange, somewhat dysfunctional childhood, my mom worked as a live-in housekeeper in a house that had lots of rules. I couldn't have friends over, couldn't watch television in the living room, and couldn't make noise when the boss was home.

The only thing I had *any* control over was food.

I earned the nickname "Moose," thanks to the class bully, due to my habit of downing two Big Macs, large fries, and a milkshake several days per week by the age of eleven. I'm not sure why he had it out for me, but Tom—a handsome boy with thick dark hair and a strut to his walk— seemed to take seriously his mission to make my life miserable.

One day, as I sat with my friend during recess doing school work, Tom again taunted me. "Hey Michelle, how does it feel to be such a fat moose?" Normally shy, even I had a breaking point! I stood up, twisted his arm behind his back, pushed him, and shouted "leave me alone!"

"Wow, Michelle is really getting heavy," a family friend whispered to my mom one day during a visit. Mortified, I hated her for being so hurtful!

A string of similar comments from others led to my first attempt to diet. At thirteen, I had no idea how to "diet." Thus began the diet "rollercoaster" I would ride for many years to come.

In Search of the Perfect Diet

My "diets" had all kinds of different rules over the years. One was focused on low fat, another on high protein. I went from not eating certain combinations of food, to *only* eating certain combinations of foods! You name it, I tried it. Finally, I managed to drop 20 pounds. While none of the boys at school seemed to notice, a boy named Chris at our family campground that summer began to flirt with me!

Fooling around with a group of friends at the lake one afternoon, he playfully picked me up and swung me around. My heart stopped, then pounded wildly. Chris was the cutest guy there! I was on a high for days! I knew then I never wanted to be heavy again. Despite my momentary resolve, however, I spent years battling the scale and continued on through endless bouts of yo-yo dieting, exercising, and obsessing over food.

Finally, by the age of 21, I thought I had it under control. It was then that I fell in love with Keith. Tall, handsome, charming and funny, he made me feel *so* good and always made me laugh.

When we met my confidence was at an all time high. But little by little he started poking fun at me for not eating a cheeseburger or chips, and he'd coerce me into skipping the gym to spend time with him. When my weight started to creep back up, he started with the comments: "You'll never look like you did when I met you."

Sadly, I started to believe it, and the binging began. During the holidays his mother made large quantities of every delicious cookie imaginable and hid them under the bed in the spare room. I couldn't stop thinking about those delightful peanut butter balls covered in chocolate or the peanut butter cookies with the Hersey's kiss sunk into the middle. I remember sneaking into the room and under the bed to snatch a cookie, feeling ashamed the whole time.

I longed to get back to the old me. I was obsessed with what I should and shouldn't eat. I woke morning after morning with tremendous guilt from last night's binge. I felt utter shame and embarrassment for my lack of control.

Each day I promised myself that today would be different. I would spend the day compiling a mental list of justifications. *One more cookie won't matter*, and *I'll start again tomorrow*, were words I lived by. Instead of admitting to myself that I was sad and lonely, I ate until I felt sick and numb. Overeating often led to fatigue. Then I'd fall asleep, only to wake and eat more as a pick-me-up.

In my mid 20's I decided to go back to college and obtain a degree in nutrition. I longed for answers to my food dilemma. It was there I discovered I had an eating disorder called compulsive overeating, and that I used food to anesthetize my feelings.

Despite all I knew about food and how our bodies processed it, I still used it in a misguided attempt to heal myself emotionally. I was oblivious to the fact that my challenges were never about the food, but rather about my inability to delve into my emotions.

Growing up there was no room for emotions; it was as if they weren't allowed. Who would have listened, anyway? And I didn't dare get angry.

While sadness was very much a part of my life, I convinced myself that—to get by—I had to put on a happy face.

Touched by an Angel

Things began to turn around when I met Lisa at a business networking event. A beautiful woman in her mid-forties with a bright smile and short blond hair, she looked like an angel. When I learned she was a life coach—a line of work I'd never heard of before—I agreed to meet her for lunch to hear more.

Drawn to work with her, I now realize my turning point occurred when I took this "leap of faith." Through her coaching, I began to recognize my negative self-talk. I'd been beating myself up for years, constantly berating myself because my thighs were too fat, my belly rolled over my pants, and my tummy wasn't flat.

At this point I convinced myself I was a failure. I'd never look like I did when I met Keith—and I just plain old wasn't good enough... Years of subconscious espionage had laid my self-esteem extremely low. I began to realize that I'd lived as a victim. Not only a victim of the world—my childhood, my relationships, etc.—but also of myself.

As my awareness grew, I asked myself how any self-respecting human being could think this way about herself and expect to be happy. With practice I began letting go of my negative self-talk and substituted kinder, gentler, more positive affirmations.

The first thing I noticed was that my binging slowed. I craved more vegetables and ate smaller portions. I began naturally to want to feed my body better not because I should, but because I felt better when I did. Simultaneously, my motivation shifted from wanting to look good to wanting to *feel* good, and exercise became more enjoyable.

For many years I let the "wild child" in me run my life. If I wasn't willing to do the hard work, how could I reap the rewards?

Along the way, I learned to set reasonable goals and to eliminate my old rationalizations to let myself off the hook. I practiced self-love and got real about where I was being too hard on myself and where I lacked discipline. I began to understand that I shouldn't let the number on the scale determine my happiness, and that I could trust myself with both my food and my life.

Previously convinced that—in order to be liked and to get what I wanted—I had to please everyone, I now felt myself getting my power back. As I began to speak more of my own truth, the food issues released themselves even more.

What I once saw as a tremendous struggle I now know was a most priceless gift.

Inspired, I decided it was time to serve others, and to help them with their own journey back to health. The freedom I now felt was too good not to share!

I began to coach and to lead weight loss seminars. Linda, one of my first clients, was anxious to join the group, but clearly wanted nothing to do with deprivation or dieting. It felt great to help bring more awareness to her life and her eating. She realized she could still enjoy the foods she loved, and ended up losing 50 pounds in less than a year!

When my clients complain, "It's easy for you to say, you don't know my situation." I look them in the eye and ask *Are you kidding?* I sit them down, explain my past, and together we begin to plan their strategy to win the weight game...

ABOUT THE AUTHOR: Michelle Marin's passion is working with individuals and groups on weight loss, stress management and other wellness related topics. A professional wellness coach and speaker, Michelle also holds an undergraduate degree in nutrition. After finding her own unique path, she achieved her ideal weight, found joy in life, and now delights in inspiring individuals to lead healthier, happier lives. Michelle leads group exercise classes, regularly teaches motivational classes at a women's prison, and leads a Breakthrough to Success course at organizations.

Michelle Marin
Your Ideal Weight, LLC
www.michellemarin.org
michelle@youridealweight.biz
860-919-6388

Motherhood:
Raising Myself Right
Margaret Moro

I remember asking God when I was four years old why He put me in a family that didn't want me or love me. I was constantly told that I couldn't do what my brothers did because I was a girl. While they did fun things, I helped my mother clean the house or visit with her sisters. When a neighborhood dad told my brother that boys were not supposed to hit girls, they were supposed to protect them, I was amazed.

As a child, the only profession that I ever considered was teaching because it fit into the family lifestyle…I could raise my children and work if I had to. Everything in my life was geared around my being a mother and having a family.

I hadn't wanted to become a mother until I was certain I could rise above the painful limits within which I was raised. Though expressive, my family of origin left me feeling both emotionally and physically vulnerable as a victim of their cultural and familial rigidity.

I didn't marry after college, and the disappointment became unbearable to my mother. I felt incomplete since I didn't have a family of my own. I clung to the idea that there had to be a better way than being like my mother. I began to experience a different lifestyle in college during the end of the 60's; one that challenged my values.

I became a marriage and family therapist to learn more about the role emotions play in our lives. As a therapist, I listened to people talk, and sometimes cry, about the pains of their childhood. They talked about how hurtful it was when they felt they weren't being seen, heard, or taken seriously.

Unmarried at 40, I had decided that raising a child alone was not for me. But when I met and married my husband at 44, the picture changed and we decided to adopt a baby girl from China. I'd always promised myself that if I had a child, I'd never consciously hurt her—bully her or treat her as an object—but respect and honor her.

I became a first time mother at the age of 47 when my husband and I adopted a Chinese baby, discarded because she was born a female. Since much of my own childhood pain occurred because I was born female in a male dominated Italian-American household and a sexist society, I identified with her immediately.

After the initial excitement of being a new mom ended, I found myself alone with my toddling daughter day after day without much support. Away for twelve hours each day commuting and working, my husband was mostly around only in the late evenings and on weekends. My own mother had passed away when I was thirty-five, and I had neither sisters nor friends my age with babies. My peers already had grandchildren my daughter's age! The mothers in our play group talked about partying while in college, as I attended my twenty-fifth college reunion.

Depressed and experiencing physical pain in my lower back, I realized that my life had changed dramatically since the days of being regarded as an authority as a psychotherapist. I felt like the definition of motherhood meant standing in the middle of a highway trying to dodge speeding cars. Childrearing keeps a mother in constant contact with her own childhood, both consciously and unconsciously. Feelings come and go from everywhere. How lucky are those women who can claim happy childhoods and wonderful mothers after which to model themselves!

I found it interesting that, as a single professional woman, I'd taken full care of myself, financially and emotionally. Capable of competently handling all aspects of my own life then, my life seemed to change when my daughter arrived. Unbeknownst to me at first, I unconsciously took on the role of "mama," and all that went with it.

Raising Her Right

I came into motherhood with an attitude of respect for my child, and an awareness that she has her own perspectives, experience, and destiny. Gia had been found and brought to the orphanage. She'd been fortunate enough to receive parents who truly wanted her, and who did not see any shame in her being female. I promised to let her evolve into her own person. She was an easy child, and I knew that most of my pain came from inside myself and had nothing to do with her.

I learned about projection and focused on self-reflection to become more conscious of my feelings in order to understand what was really going on. If I felt anger at Gia, was it about her or about me? If I was disappointed in her, from where did this disappointment *really* stem? Was it about her or about me, or about my own mother's disappointment in me?

And what if she didn't want what I was offering? What if she didn't do what I wanted her to do? How do I feel about her exercising her right to say no? It required much self-reflection on my part in order for me to take responsibility for myself and to keep my promises to her and to me.

I wanted her to possess a high level of self esteem, to have many opportunities from which to choose, and to feel emotionally supported. I wanted her to grow up knowing she could do *anything*, rather than just what was within the cultural and familial limits that had bound me. Like many parents, I desired more for my daughter than what I'd received in my own childhood.

Despite my progress, I knew I still needed more support. I began to participate in The Journey, an organization built on teaching processes to heal emotional pain. Through this process I began to reconnect with myself and surpass where I left myself before I took on the role of "mama."

At a workshop, when asked the question "what beliefs do you hold as a woman that no longer serve you? My answer surfaced instantly: FAMILY FIRST! I immediately recognized that—as soon as I was handed my baby—I unconsciously and automatically fell into the role of "mama." And, just as with my mother, *my* needs became secondary or non-existent.

Victimized by the cultural roles thrust upon and instilled in me, I automatically accepted that the role of "mama" meant that I was supposed to take responsibility for the emotional, physical, and organizational well-being of the family. Playing the role of "mama" did not allow me to pursue my own needs and therefore, my joy. Being a mama was supposed to be my joy, and I found I needed more.

I began to reclaim myself. First I knew I had to become aware of my limiting cultural beliefs, and to change them into empowering beliefs; beliefs that served *me*. I needed to be my authentic self, not inflated or deflated, not victimized by roles—and to no longer wait for someone to rescue me. As I took full responsibility for myself, physically, spiritually, and financially, I discovered I had more energy. I realized I could make choices, decide what I wanted and strategize how to get it, and all the while enjoy having a family.

Secondly, I learn from my daughter. Gia, now 14, is her own person. She does not eat like a kid who was reminded about the "starving children of the world" so many nights at the dinner table. Instead, she's been given the freedom to eat what is right for her. This, in turn, frees *me* from that place inside that says food can't be wasted, and now I have more choices as well.

She does what she truly loves; cheerleading, singing, creating on her computer, curling her straight hair. She takes her time as she puts on makeup, rests, or does nothing at all. Through her, I am granted the same freedoms; to take time with myself and to find out what I love. I now give myself time to be creative, to sing out loud, and to explore my world.

Although I did explore my world during my single years, as "mama" I did not give myself that luxury. Now, however, I am a mama *and* a person; I've taken myself out of the confines of the role in which I was raised. Now, instead, I am a person who happens to be a mother.

My legacy to Gia lies with my ability to give her the gift of authenticity. It's OK for her to grow up and not dream *only* of having a family, as I did. Instead, I can teach her to understand that she can be open to exploring the world, and that she does not have to be thrust into any kind of rigid role. And, best of all, she can learn to trust her intuition. At 14, she continues to unfold and believes she can do whatever is right for her. She knows she is smart and beautiful. Sometimes, I am in awe of her.

I ask myself whether or not motherhood has transformed me? Still not a "kid" person, I nevertheless love and respect my child. As I raise her right, I continue to raise myself right, because it's never too late. I continue to explore my own creativity, to figure out exactly what I want to be when I grow up, as the cliché goes...I'm no longer a therapist since, for me, that is an extension of caretaking. Even though I have a Ph.D., I still consider myself a student.

Soon enough, Gia will leave the nest, and I will embrace *that* next stage in my life. When the time comes, I know my curiosity will still lead me, as my life continues to unfold in its myriad unimaginable ways. For now the complex, yet simple, equation remains: I am her mother, she is my teacher; we both transform each other through our love...

ABOUT THE AUTHOR: Margaret Moro, Ph.D., has been a Marriage and Family Therapist in private practice since 1986. Her areas of specialty have included recovery from addictions, childhood abuse and relationships. She has been a workshop creator and presenter, a trainer, an adjunct instructor at three colleges, and a retreat leader for women. She is certified as a Journey Practitioner and a Conscious Leadership Coach through The Journey (TM). She is the owner of Y Weight, LLC, where she combines her skills and experience in helping relieve people from whatever is weighing them down.

Margaret V Moro, Ph.D.
mvmoro@verizon.net
732 673-0139

The Personal Brand of ME
Or How to be Who You are Without Apology
Lethia Owens

Just as I entered the bathroom stall and closed the door, I heard two women come into the ladies room behind me. "Have you met Lethia Owens yet?" one of the ladies asked the other. Wow, I thought, they're talking about me! I eagerly peeped through the crack in the door waiting for the reply.

I followed their movements intensely as I strained to see them through the door crack and to hear every word they would share about how nice it was to meet me. To my surprise, I heard the second woman respond, without hesitation, "Yes I have! *Who* does she think she is?"

At that moment, my heart sank and hit the toilet, or at least that's what it felt like! To avoid their embarrassment—should they discover me in the room—I climbed on top of the toilet and struggled to keep my balance, as I placed my hands on each side of the wall for support and pretended I was invisible.

This was one of my first experiences connecting with new people in my community. I'd developed the desire to connect more powerfully to my community and the people within it. For too long, my life revolved only around a close knit circle of family, friends and co-workers. I'd come to the women's networking group, eWomenNetwork, in St. Louis, MO, to meet other women who, like me, were on their journey to living their dreams.

I've always been a talker, and I'd excitedly shared my dreams with anyone who would listen. I was having so much fun that I barely came up for air. It was when I decided to take a break from all of the excitement that I made my way to the ladies room for what I'd assumed would be a quick pit stop.

Little did I know I'd end up perched on a toilet pretending to be invisible! As soon as the ladies left, I exited the stall and faced the disappointed version of myself looking back at me in the mirror. "How could they say those things about me when they don't even know me?" I wondered.

It suddenly became clear to me that perception is *everything*. I didn't understand that others *don't* perceive me in the same way that I perceive myself. Rather, others make decisions based not on *my* perception of *myself*, but on how *they* perceive me!

Determined not to let this incident shake me, I quickly decided that my response should be to take a closer look at what would eventually become my "personal brand." After all, these ladies didn't even know me—I wasn't going to let their words hurt me.

Instead, I decided to send out my first "personal brand" assessment to solicit feedback from my friends, peers, clients, mentors, and supervisor to get a better idea of what people actually thought about me.

If anyone had asked me to describe myself, I would have said that I'm kind, tenacious, focused, driven, and that I get back up any time I fall. However, when I got my survey results back, the feedback was overwhelmingly clear. To my surprise, these results painted a very different picture.

The respondents overwhelmingly shared that they saw me as: demanding, controlling, always thinking I'm right, and as a person who never shuts up, and never says she's sorry. My first thought was "how could they all be so wrong?"

Okay, so they *weren't* all wrong. I had to face the fact that the perception I had in my head about who I am is so very different from the perception that others hold in their head about my "personal brand."

Damage Control

The question now was how do I go about repairing my damaged

brand? I realized that my first step was to accept the reality of my situation, and embrace the feedback. I could have ignored the feedback but I knew that wouldn't serve me well. In addition, I wanted to put in place a plan to improve the areas that had turned into "brand killers." In short, I wanted to better understand why people with whom I worked and had relationships perceived me the way they did.

You see, I'd become a person I didn't love. I had bought houses, cars and things I couldn't afford to try to impress people I didn't even like. And all in the name of attempting to prove that I was *good enough*.

As I sat in my office, as a leader in State Farm Insurance Company's information technology department, I reflected on my "survey's" feedback. Suddenly, a memory floated up from my past—something that had happened when I was fourteen years old that I began to realize had always held me back from attaining my full potential in life.

I came to realize that this pivotal event is what caused me to behave the way I did. At the age of fourteen I dropped out of high school due to my pregnancy. When I went to tell my homeroom teacher Mr. Wilder that I'd be leaving his class, he looked at me over the top of his thin wire-framed glasses and sneered "You'll never amount to anything." It was like someone kicked me in the gut. Feelings of shame and judgment rushed over me. I left his class that day with my head hung low, doubting my future and devastated that I had disappointed him.

Months later, after my daughter was born, I remember wondering what it would feel like to hold my high school diploma in my hand, and to have my parents celebrate my graduation from high school. This then became my dream, and my dream became my intention. Three years later, I walked across the stage on graduation day as an honor graduate with a full academic scholarship. I went on to graduate from college with a computer science degree, a Chartered Life Underwriter designation and a Masters in Managerial Leadership.

Who Says You Can't Go Home?

Sitting at my desk at State Farm, with a clearer understanding of why people perceived me the way they do, I realized it was time to visit Mr.

Wilder. So I planned my trip home and soon found myself driving 843 miles across three states to say "hi" to him! When I returned to Westover High School in my hometown of Albany, Georgia, I marched into the guidance counselors' office to ask if Mr. Wilder was still in room 223.

The counselor leaned over the desk and whispered to me, "Mr. Wilder is no longer with us…he committed suicide two years ago." I sat there in stunned silence for a few minutes and contemplated my next step. I mean, I had driven all this way to confront the man who had so profoundly altered the course of my life… suddenly I understood that hurt people sometimes hurt people, but that what Mr. Wilder had said to me that day had very little to do with *me,* and more to do with where he was in his own life.

I rose from my seat with renewed will and conviction, thanked the guidance counselor for her time, and proceeded to room 223. The room was dark and empty, and I stood outside in the hall for a few minutes. I remembered so clearly the damp smell of teenage body odor and the sounds of giggling, shuffling, and activity as students rushed to class. I stepped into the classroom, turned on the lights, and returned to the very spot in which Mr. Wilder had spoken his words to me. I closed my eyes, stretched out my hands and said, "Mr. Wilder, you were wrong about me!" Then I quietly exited the room and returned to my car, a new woman.

Through this experience I shed the need to please other people, and realized that nothing and no one could validate my own self worth but *me.* Already an awesomely wonderful creation of God almighty, all I need do each day is make him proud by being who he'd created me to be.

Now every night before bed I ask myself two questions: "Lethia, have you done your best today?" The answer is often yes. Then I ask "Lethia, can you do better tomorrow?" And the answer is ALWAYS yes.

Through this journey of self-discovery I've learned that it's critical to my success and survival to be true to myself. Now that I am comfortable being who I am on purpose and without apology, I am bigger, more powerful, and more valuable than what anyone in my past may have tried to make me believe…and now my own "personal brand" comes across the same to others as does to me.

ABOUT THE AUTHOR: Lethia is the president and CEO of Lethia Owens International, Inc. and is internationally recognized as a personal branding and social media strategist, speaker, author and coach. She uses high value content, dynamic keynote presentations and engaging training programs to show others they too can achieve extraordinary results if they have the right skills and attitude. Lethia is a highly sought after speaker, coach and consultant. Her dynamic message on has inspired thousands of professionals across the globe in 49 of the 50 United States and also in Dubai UAE, London, Muscat, Bahrain, San Juan Puerto Rico and Canada. www.LethiaOwens.com

Lethia Owens
www.LethiaOwens.com
lethia@lethiaowens.com
636-244-5041

Welcome to My Garden
Michele Santo

Years ago I had an obsession. It was saving people. If they gave a Nobel Peace Prize for always putting self last, I would have collected quite a few. Friends confided in me, strangers told me everything…I must have had "tell me your problems—no *really!*" written all over my face.

At the time, selflessness was my thing. I wrote it off as a virtue. Relationships with men were like sale rack jeans—irresistible at first, but then I'd take them home and discover a hole in the crotch. Crap! With regular wear, depressed and twisted personalities unraveled.

I admit their dysfunction intrigued me. I didn't view the world as bad or good. I acknowledged only opportunities. And when things seemed to fall apart, I saw it only as a "lesson," a chance to grow.

My relationship with Page outlived its expiration date. We met in Art class. Creativity, design and NYC adventures kept us together for four and a half years, as we both tried desperately to make it work. From the outside, we made an attractive couple, but our communication styles didn't mesh.

He drove me to my design gig one afternoon. I don't recall our conversation, but I'm sure I was hyper-focusing on something irrelevant when he blurted out, "you're worthless!" Ummm…was that his idea of a Zen proverb? Freak you, dude!

I stormed out of his car sobbing hysterically. I could barely catch my breath. The knot in my stomach would only have gotten worse had I fled home. So I went to my best friend's mom's house. "I'm sorry to barge in, Mrs. Glo, but I need to talk!" She hugged me and questioned the tears. "My boyfriend just told me I'm WORTHLESS!? How could he say that? He's supposed to love me!"

"Oh, Michele, that's not true. I don't know what he was thinking! You're smart and beautiful. Plus you have a jade ring on your finger." I followed her gaze and noticed my rectangular stone embellished with marcasite. "Green is for nature, spring time and growth! You should always wear that ring!" My insides smiled. She knew what was up!

The next guy was a black belt in karate. We met through a friend at a pool hall. He was a smooth talker and a total mama's boy.

We cooked at home often. So that Labor Day it was a treat to wine and dine—until we got home. Snuggling up to a movie was the plan. When we arrived at his parent's house, he wandered off to chat with his mom. Waiting for a half hour was awkward. Was he dating his mother or me?

When he reappeared, I asked, "What took you so long? I thought we were gonna watch a movie?" He replied, "I like to check in when I come home. I'm not an asshole like your brother!" Whoa, no one talks smack about my family. And my bro is *not* a jerk, so I slapped him.

Not the wisest decision. He forcefully grabbed my arms and got in my face. Breathing down my neck, he said, "You know I can throw you down the steps right now!" I thrust his body away from me and screamed "Stop it! Get the hell off me!"

I dropped to the ground in shock when he punched me in the nose. Is this seriously happening? Who *is* this guy? His parents rushed in. Now his mother was in my face, yelling, "Get your pretty ass up and *get out of this house!*" Apparently, the apple didn't fall far from the tree.

Looking away, I blared, "Can ya give me a freakin' minute? Your son just *hit me in the face!*" She wouldn't back off. So I stood up, looked her in the eye and said, "Oh, I'm outta here alright! Congratulations, Jayne, you've created a menace!" and pointed to her son, who cowered behind his father. The look of righteousness on his face was unbelievable, as if I was the bad guy. I walked out completely speechless.

A few years later, I decided to give online dating a shot. What the hey! Meeting men I wouldn't bump into on the street was interesting. Oddly enough, the one who lived three hundred miles away struck my fancy.

Initially I suggested friendship. Long emails became phone calls, which unfolded into a year-long, long distance relationship. We met up every two weeks, when one of us either drove or flew to New York City, Massachusetts, New Jersey, Pennsylvania, Burlington or Montreal. Although a blast, it wasn't real life.

I was sure it was love. The subject of marriage came up quickly. I moved to Vermont to get to know the day-to-day J. As soon as I carried my last bag in the door, my intuition whispered "you're not safe here." There was no tangible reason why, yet I didn't unpack for seven days.

A student at the Institute for Integrative Nutrition in New York City, I was excited to become a health coach, and fascinated by fitness, nutrition and anything holistic! During this time, I worked remotely for them. I also attended Meetups to make friends. I'd pretend Lake Champlain was the Jersey Shore. It wasn't.

J and I split rent and groceries. His debt was six figures deep. I assumed my frugal ways would help straighten that out. He just dug himself deeper into credit card craziness. We fought. Loneliness hung over me like a dark cloud.

One evening J's college buddy called up. I could not believe what I overheard. He hadn't paid the rent since April! It was now September. I moved there in June. What the flip happened to my three months of paid rent money?

I confronted him. Furious and betrayed didn't do me justice! He proceeded to tell me he was in some virtual hell. I said, "No shit! The rent is overdue, you just got fired, and we're not getting along. What are you going to do?" "I want you to leave," was his answer. It felt like a cop out so he wouldn't have to tell me the whole truth. I assured him we would never speak again. He didn't care.

"Well, then you need to leave the apartment now so I can pack my things," I requested. He walked out and I filled my suitcases in a New York minute. It was a seven hour drive home and I was determined to fit everything into my two-door Honda Civic. I shoved two and a half carloads of my stuff into every crevice of that car. My knees were up to the steering wheel but I couldn't wait to get home.

Before merging onto I-95 South, I updated my Facebook status to single, and wrote "returning to my home." My friends called off the hook. For three hundred miles straight I was in good company. Never once did I look back.

The New Me

My homecoming inspired a new appreciation for New Jersey. I had no clue how spoiled I'd been here! Great food, music, diversity, opportunity, and entertainment—it was *all* here!

I slowly began to realize that my attraction to these relationships was no accident. Each one of them was like an "assignment" to heal. But still I avoided tending my own garden.

After the final, "What was I thinking relationship?" I suffered from insomnia, dehydration and adrenal fatigue. Merely getting out of bed and walking exhausted me. I used to jog, hike, and downward dog. Something was seriously off.

The Universe made it abundantly clear that if I gave my energy away then zapped is how I'd feel. I was beyond drained and disconnected from the beautiful blue-eyed woman in the mirror. Thankfully I was a health coach, so I decided to become my own client.

Green smoothies became my morning ritual. I'd race downstairs to see what I could mix up. Drinking fresh fruits and greens made me feel so alive! My skin started to glow! I learned how to tune into what my body needed but hadn't appreciated before. In fact, my body was *always* speaking to me.

My rendezvous with healthy cooking began. It was magical to pick veggies and spices from the garden and throw something together. Sure, some dishes tasted bland at first, but they pleased me because I made them with love. Each re-creation was tastier. Spices were a lifesaver!

Exercise at The Training Rim finally became consistent. My body transformed into my dream physique—Wow! It *is* really possible! Meditation became my saving grace. I learned how to quiet the mind chatter. I found an amazing meditation group at Soulful Awakenings in Belmar, where I've grown exponentially. They're now like my second family—I love them so much!

I dug out my old acrylics, as my desire to paint resurfaced. Bright colors, textures and words turned me on! I'd crammed my creativity painfully into journal pages for years, but now I realized I'd neglected my art, such a natural part of my being.

Wow, how divine to play with paint again! It's hard to explain the connection to God as an artist. When the paintbrush is in my hand, I'm fully connected to the Universe. Divine energy channels through me and pours out onto the canvas.

It's a place of total freedom, like dancing or a runner's high. I allowed myself to be completely present in the moment. Nothing is more liberating!

I kept painting the same four words: "Let go, let God." They spilled out of me as my hand danced across the canvas. The Universe whispered to me not to worry. With every stroke, I quieted. With every repetition, I trusted. I knew the worst was behind me and the best was happening now.

A light bulb went off. I understood in a flash there was no need to quest after love, when the seed was buried deep within. Everything I'd ever searched for in the dark lit up inside me, calling for my attention. Well hello, Michele, welcome to your garden! It's time to co-create whatever you want! You know the world ain't seen nothin' yet! Who loves ya, gorgeous? *I sure do!*

ABOUT THE AUTHOR: Michele Santo is the Health Coach to women who are reinventing their lives. She helps them cook, lose weight and create more energy. Her philosophy is that diet and lifestyle change everything from relationships, life purpose and overall happiness. She received her training at Integrative Nutrition in N.Y.C. and offers private and group health coaching and cooking classes. Michele is known for her infectious laugh and compassionate spirit. She is a writer, nature lover and smoothie freak. Her favorite quote is, "Our deepest fear is not that we are inadequate. Our deepest fear is that we are powerful beyond measure."

Michele Santo
www.MicheleSanto.com
Michele@MicheleSanto.com
908-770-9789

Too Young to Die
Carmela Schiano

Thrown back against the driver's seat, blinded by the reflection of the lights, my head reeled as the car rolled over and over and tumbled 25 feet down the ravine. Time seemed to stand still as I felt the cold December night air enter my car. Outside it was totally black. It was freezing; my wet silk blouse stuck to me, and the cold ran up my entire body. I clutched at myself just to see if I was still in one piece.

All of a sudden I felt water in my car. My seatbelt on, I was stuck. The belt pressed tighter and tighter on my body. I couldn't move. Panic set in as I realized I couldn't get out of my car. Tears rolled downed my cheeks as I thought back over the past 29 years of my life. How did I get here? Where am I? Will anyone find me? Am I going to die? Is *this* where my life ends?

Suddenly my obituary flashed before my eyes:

"Beloved daughter and not so beloved ex-wife, first generation 29 year-old Italian American educated for twelve years by the nuns, a sheltered, middle child with a brother a year and a day older, an "Ugly Betty" plain Jane with no self-esteem and no self-confidence, may she rest in peace."

Arrivederci Roma!

My life started in New York, a first generation Italian American born in South Brooklyn to two Italian immigrants from Naples Italy. This neighborhood by the waterfront, in sight of the two beautiful towers that once stood tall, now gone, used to be called Red Hook, but is now known as Carroll Gardens.

My father, handsome and dark haired, raised in Italy, traveled to the U.S, the land of opportunity, at the age of 18, following his Dad. My mom, slim and brunette, a natural beauty, was also 18 when she boarded a ship in Italy to the U.S. with her three younger siblings. What courage it took for them both, especially my mom, who took responsibility for her younger siblings at such an early age.

My parents met soon after arriving in the States. It seemed like love at first sight. Within six months, they were off to Niagara Falls for their honeymoon.

Week after week on Tuesdays my uncles closed their pizzerias and took the day off to spend with their families. My parents, brother, aunts, uncles and cousins would drive to the Brooklyn ferry on 69th street and head to Staten Island.

For me it was a vacation, a picnic at the beach. Each uncle and aunt would make his or her favorite dish, and my mom would make her specialties, spaghetti pie and potato croquettes that were to die for. Surrounded by great Italian food, this was my vacation from Carroll Street in downtown Brooklyn. To me, the ferry was like a cruise ship and the destination was like a faraway land with sandy beaches, a playground, and a picnic area.

Holidays were much the same. The only difference is that they took place at the pizzerias after they closed to the public. Family life was great for eight years. Concrete playground, eerie gates, fist ball, running bases, hopscotch, Good Humor trucks, panelle sandwiches, and girls hanging out on the street corners, watching the boys go by.

The Old Country

Despite these wonderful memories, what stayed in my mind and haunted me for years was my father's voice saying "children are to be seen and not heard." Though a frequently used phrase by parents in the 1950s, to me it meant that children were nothing but a burden.

One night, the black and white TV off, finished with my homework, the phone rang. My mother answered, and after a few moments tears started rolling down her cheeks.

Shocking news from my father—he didn't want to come home!

Terrified, I immediately felt abandoned. How would we survive without a dad? Who'll pay the rent and buy the food? Who will care for us? As much as I was afraid of my controlling, domineering dad, or that voice, I was too young to survive alone.

Then the shame sank in, followed by a sense of hopelessness. What will the neighbors say? What will my friends think? My father stayed away and my mom cried constantly. Despite the shame, I looked forward to school as a way to escape the pain I felt at home. There was no yelling, no cursing. I felt safe. I could still be a child in school.

When I came home from school, I remembered that dad was gone, that he no longer cared for us. We needed money for food and rent. We needed to find out where he was, and call him and get him back!

My dad came and went throughout my life. One day a week, on the weekend, we had to visit him at a place called The Burger Flame. I hated those visits. While my friends went to the movies or on outings with friends, I had to disappear and lie about where I was going. The guilt and shame festered inside me.

But I pretended everything was perfect. We lived behind closed doors, closed windows, but my father's voice still haunted me. And I was never able to tell anyone the truth. I made it through high school without any serious boyfriends. I didn't want to get close to anyone; I always feared what they might find out, or what I might need to tell them.

At sixteen, as I planned to make my selections for college, my dad unexpectedly showed up at the apartment with two of his friends' brothers in tow. He'd brought them to me so they could have a look at his daughter in order to marry her off! He paraded them by me as though I was a dress hanging in a store window he hoped one of them might choose to buy!

Instead of proudly sending his daughter off to college in this new land of opportunity, my father clearly fell back into his "old-country" attitude. We don't send our women to college, we just marry them off—they should be seen and not heard, just like our children…I would have been shocked, but I'd already 'been there' the night the phone rang and he'd decided never to come home again.

Needless to say, I did not marry any of those men. However, I did go to college and pay my own way, thanks to my mom and my aunt's support. And I worked throughout both high school and college.

One night I went on a blind date with a young man in my neighborhood. We ended up dating for two years; things seemed fine until a few days before the wedding.

Scheduled for a dental cleaning, (I wanted a bright smile for my wedding pictures!), I arrived at the dentist's office with no worries. When the dentist accidentally dropped the drill on me, red blood gushed from my lip. They tried to stop the bleeding, and when I heard them shouting that I might need stitches I started to faint.

I had the office call my boyfriend, but he didn't come. He was too busy with the boys!

The real problems began within a month after the wedding. It was like living with a total stranger. He lost his job and became a different person—moody, domineering, and controlling. He ridiculed me by calling me names and humiliating me.

I cooked, cleaned and ironed his underwear, as he yelled and threw things at me. I was threatened, humiliated, and put down. Afraid for my life, I sought the help of counselors, and left. But the guilt and shame of divorce in a Catholic family came with me.

"In All Thy Ways Acknowledge Him and He Shall Direct Thy Paths" Proverbs 3:6

"Hello! Is anyone down there?"

"Yes, yes, it's me! I'm alive! Please help!"

Still stuck in the car at the bottom of the ravine, wet, cold and scared out of my mind, I never imagined that a car accident on my way home from Albany would change my life forever. Trapped there, I prayed and prayed and prayed, until I knew God visited me and made it clear that I was being given another chance to truly live my life.

Frank, a born again preacher, found me. He'd seen a light and passed it by, but twenty minutes down the road something compelled him to return. When he'd turned around and reached the spot, he got out of his car, stood by the ledge, and looked down 25 feet into the ravine. There were the wheels of my car spinning futilely in the water.

From that day forward, I accepted my mission to invite God back into my life. And I knew in my heart he would be with me forever. The rest, as they say, was a dream come true. I found a man I could trust and love, and I married him. That was 25 years ago...

I forgave those whom I allowed to control me. I regained my power, and I stay focused on today and live in the moment. I now live my life the way I know it is intended to be—without shame, free of guilt and worry—because I know it *is* possible to forgive others, to recover, and move forward to new beginnings…

"The secret of health for both mind and body is not to mourn for the past, nor to worry about the future, but to live the present moment wisely and earnestly!" Siddhartha Gautama

"Happiness is not something readymade; it comes from your own actions." Dalia Lama XIV

I am a gift from God and blessed to be here living each day!

ABOUT THE AUTHOR: Certified as a Professional Life and Business Coach by the Institute for Professional Excellence in Coaching (iPEC), Carmela helps empower her clients to achieve their personal and professional goals through proven inspirational and coaching techniques. Carmela draws on her experience as a New York City teacher and day care director, an educational consultant, and as the Northeast Regional Sales Manager of the Lyons Group, Inc., where she introduced and managed the sale of "Barney the Dinosaur" products in 19 northeastern states. Carmela lives in New York City with her husband and daughter, a professional ballerina.

Carmela Schiano
Live Free Coaching
www.livefreecoaching.com
carmela@livefreecoaching.com
917-592-7241

PART TWO

Transformation Through Adversity

"No pessimist ever discovered the secrets of the stars,
or sailed to an uncharted land,
or opened a new heaven to the human spirit"
~ Helen Keller

The Wake Up Call

Ferlinda Almonte

That's it! I'm retailed out, I'm changing careers! That was my decision after my boss informed me by phone one morning that my company had gone under. I had one hour to pick up my personal belongings, and surrender my keys!

This chilling news served as a repeat of the terse call I'd received a year earlier from my then vice president at my place of employment. "Ferlie, effective immediately, stop selling shoes, turn off the lights and lock the doors—*now!*" she commanded. "The company failed to get financing from investors and decided to close shop."

And only twelve months before *that*, I'd learned I was a casualty at the chic, privately owned eyeglass store where I worked, when budget cuts and a major corporate merger took their toll on my position.

So, armed with a license in respiratory therapy and a shattered belief in the U.S. retail economy, I ventured back into the more secure world of healthcare. Unfortunately, I felt I did not belong in a hospital setting. The plight of critically ill patients proved too emotionally draining for me.

I managed to stumble into a pulmonary function testing tech job that utilized my respiratory therapy license in a more upbeat environment.

I loved this new job! I found total enjoyment performing breathing tests on patients. Patients always greeted me with a smile when I called them from the waiting room and told them I was going to take their breaths away—literally! All I needed were pom-poms as I instructed them fill their lungs with air and blow really hard, and to keep on blowing until they were empty. I was known as the "blow girl!"

But my joy was short lived. One of the frequent tests I performed on patients was methacholine challenge, a diagnostic test for asthma. The test induced asthma in patients when they inhaled methacholine, and we measured their responses to increased dosages of this drug.

Because I inhaled the by-product of methacholine in a tight, non-ventilated room during the two years that I worked there, I repeatedly complained to the doctors and office manager of the increasing tightening of my airways, and requested that ventilation be installed.

But they continually denied my requests, and dismissed my concerns by telling me that methacholine dissipates in the air. I needed several maintenance inhalers and was given a subcutaneous biotech drug that cost $30,000 a year to control my symptoms.

Unfortunately, I was not smart enough to demand ventilation be installed, or to remove myself from that toxic environment. No one heeded the warning signs.

Two years later, I found myself in the emergency room fighting for my life. Nearly intubated, my lung function had been severely compromised by the hazardous exposure. Hospitalized twice in three years for over a week with status asthmaticus—an acute exacerbation of asthma that does not respond to standard treatments of bronchodilators and steroids—each time I ended up on disability for six months and spent many hours frequenting several different doctor's offices.

I struggled each day with progressive tightening of the airways, labored breathing, and chest pain from relentless coughing and wheezing. My risk for respiratory failure elevated, my lower lobes collapsed, and my immune system completely shut down from all the steroids. I was left helpless, debilitated, and depressed for months.

All I Need is the Air that I Breathe…

I couldn't walk five feet without gasping desperately for air, turning blue, and feeling like I was drowning. Confined to my home, even a slight change in temperature closed my airways and led to a massive asthma exacerbation. My head would explode in pain and my stomach felt like it was on fire.

No specialist knew how to treat me. Several doctors thought I was nuts. They assumed I knew too much and probably thought I was hypochondriacally fabricating my symptoms. One doctor even advised me to seek out a pulmonary specialist in an academic institution so that I could share my unique case with others. And, on my way out, he gave me a prescription for Xanax and told me to please let him know the outcome. I did not fill it.

Then I found my way to a Harvard-trained pulmonologist in New York, who listened to me intently and patiently. "You have a problem that most patients have—your doctors *don't* listen," he said kindly. "You see, the more symptoms you tell them about, the more they have to fix," he explained. "You have to find a doctor with whom you can communicate."

He told me to lie down on the exam table and open my mouth. Then he touched something in the back of my throat that set me off into an acute asthma attack, instant headache, and non-stop burping episode right before his eyes.

I wheezed like crazy and frantically reached for my inhaler. He told me it wouldn't help, and ignored my wild spasms for several minutes until I got tired and slowly calmed down. Still wheezing, and with tears rolling down my puffy cheeks, he then proceeded to explain that I had a hyper-reactive airway and vagus nerve, and that no amount of preventive medicine could save me once the nerve was triggered.

It will act on its own, and you could die at any time, he continued calmly. The only way to save yourself is to relax, which is admittedly not easy when you're in a panic and gasping for air, he acknowledged. He looked defeated and his body slouched forward, arms resting on his legs, when he said to me "I do not want to scare you, but it concerns me." Wow, my doctor was scared for *me*.

Not yet cleared to go back to work, I was sent to a neurologist. Unsure which was scarier—the thought of struggling to breathe or of going flat broke—I consulted the neurologist. Armed with optimism and prayers for a miracle, I found an angel in my neurologist, who successfully experimented with an anti-seizure drug to control the sensitivity of my vagus nerve and prevented closure of my airways.

Meanwhile, I sued the company that recklessly exposed me to the hazardous conditions, but the small settlement from worker's compensation did not prove enough to pay for the freedom and joy of living I'd lost.

The doctors' determined I'd been left with permanent lung damage. I wanted the old, healthy me back; the Ferlie who danced and sang for hours, the energizer who enjoyed the outdoors without restriction. Wishful thinking, I thought, and realized simultaneously I can't stop living just because of my newly imposed restrictions.

Severely bloated, I looked like an Asian blimp on Macy's Thanksgiving parade because of the massive doses of life saving steroids I was forced to take. I watched my friends unsuccessfully conceal their pity and horror when they saw me come out of hibernation.

Steroids had forced my appetite through the roof. As I made my seventh trip to the buffet at a local restaurant, a casual friend I'd run into blurted out "Oh hi! I didn't know you're pregnant!" How priceless was the look of horror on her face when I told her I wasn't pregnant...but hey, I had a choice. I could be a skinny corpse, or take the steroids, and be alive and fat!

Lord, Please Show Me the Way...

I looked in the mirror and saw hope in the image of my young child behind me. I saw a damn good reason to fight for my life. The decision was easy, and God then showed me the way to make a fabulous comeback!

I landed a job in pharmaceutical sales specializing in a respiratory drug portfolio. How perfect! A respiratory therapist *and* bad asthmatic selling respiratory drugs? No brainer—I was a natural!

I met the most amazing people and learned so much while selling these drugs, but my joy was cut short due to corporate restructuring—yet again!

Within the next year, I attended a SHIFT networking event. I dropped my business card in a raffle for Soul Purpose to Prosperity life coaching sessions and found out that God wasted no time in responding to my plea!

My name was drawn from the bowl of business cards as the winner. Curious how much I really wanted or needed the life coaching, the sponsoring life coach dropped my card back in the bowl, and—as fate would have it—picked my name again. It was Divine Intervention.

During the following eight weeks of life coaching, we peeled my layers until I was raw and my soul opened to its true calling. I became aware that there's another choice other than the traditional mentality of "go to college, get a degree, and work for a Fortune 500 company" under which I was raised.

Nowhere in that philosophy could I find a way to manifest my passions successfully; only a way to be victimized again and again by its rigid structure, robotic expectations, and heartless treatment of people reduced to numbers and used as instruments only to increase corporate revenues.

Companies no longer seem to care that people currently feel extremely vulnerable and anxious about their job security. It wasn't until I separated from corporate life that I discovered I could make people happy, and feel fabulous about themselves, without having to always worry about my future.

Through this journey, the wiser, stronger, passionate Ferlilicious person in me was conceived, and the image consultant in me was born.

I wasted no time and enrolled in image intensive courses, got my certificate, and registered my business. I also revived my karaoke DJ/emcee business, and now help unleash the "bling" in the lives I touch though image makeovers, and bring out the inner rock star in us!

The magnificent synergy of faith, prayers, healing power of love, and the genius of medicine combined lead to my transformation, and gave me my health and life back. I now possess a deep sense of clarity about my true calling: to provide a life changing, empowering and entertaining experience for many others.

Now the tide has turned in my favor. No longer awakened by calls of job losses, the only wake up calls I get are about living my own greatness, through my own fearless, joyful brilliance!

ABOUT THE AUTHOR: Ferlinda Almonte considers herself a multi-talented survivor extraordinaire—Philippine-born, she made her way to America with $120 in her pocket 27 years ago. A BSBA graduate, she's a certified image consultant, the chief entertainment officer of Party Pooper Busters, and a respiratory therapist. She also worked as a clinical instructor, and in upscale retail sales management & pharmaceutical sales, where she was a consistent top performer for more than 20 years. Ferlie's mission "to unleash the *bling* in you!" is born of her successful navigation of many of life's harsh adversities, which she's turned into glittering opportunities for empowerment, wisdom & inspiration.

Ferlinda "Ferlie" R. Almonte
Jemage Image Consulting
Party Pooper Busters
ferliealmonte@yahoo.com
201-994-5617

The Best Things in Life are Free

Deborah Rae Arrigo

Mrs. A, you ought to go home and get some rest. It will be hours before we know anything. We can call you." The nurse was kind, but going home was not an option. I wanted to stay close in case the doctor needed me. Besides, being steps away from Joe made me feel closer.

I looked over my shoulder and caught a glimpse of my father-in-law sleeping peacefully in the chair behind me. How could he rest? His son was undergoing a third surgery, one of the first of its kind, and the outcome was uncertain.

Joe and I never imagined that an ear filled with liquid would end up an ear engulfed by a life threatening tumor. After the liquid dried it became evident there was a cyst on the eardrum. The first surgery was short but unsuccessful. Afterwards, he experienced extreme mood swings and horrendous headaches. He was unable to work.

The doctors regrouped and planned a second surgery several weeks later, only to find they had disturbed an unknown monster in his head and were now unable to undo what they had done. A misdiagnosed problem left the roots of his tumor stretched in all directions and growing like a grapevine through his face and up toward his brain!

No longer even able to stand, Joe cried out in tortured pain. Delirious, he'd scream and thrash his head from side to side, until he began to receive regular shots of morphine. I worried he'd become addicted, or worse, that this awful thing they'd disturbed might become more enraged! Was it possible?

I called the specialist and, barely able to speak, was totally unprepared for what I heard. "If you can get your husband transferred here within the next 72 hours he may have a chance of recovering from paralysis."

To transport Joe to the UVA Hospital, I needed to come up with five thousand dollars for an emergency ambulate with a private nurse to escort him on the three hour trip. It was already midnight when I'd gotten through to the doctor. Our resources were limited and time was of the essence for Joe's for survival.

Now here we were, seven hours into his third surgery. Worry, anticipation, anxiety, tears, stress and a heavy sad heart accompanied me on this journey. I wondered when it would be over, if everything was OK, if there were complications…dear God, don't let him die, I prayed. Our two baby girls need their daddy, I need him—we all need him!

Suddenly I leaped out of the chair, grabbed my left ear, and yelled, "Oh my God! They're sewing Joe's ear now! I can feel it!" My father-in-law awoke, dazed. "I think the doctor's almost finished with Joe's surgery. I can feel excruciating pain behind my ear! I'm sure of it, it feels like a knife." I kept my hand over my ear as if to make the pain go away.

My father in law didn't believe my mental telepathy. Still another hour passed. Finally a nurse appeared in the door. "He's fine," she reported. "He's resting now and on his way to his room from recovery."

When I first walked into the room and saw the white bandage around Joe's head, the intravenous in his arm, and bandages over his ear, I was frightened. Stepping closer, I touched his hand and he squeezed mine so I knew he was aware I was there. I bent over and kissed his hand. I told him I loved him, and silently said a prayer to thank the angels above. Joe had beaten the odds.

All Things Considered…

"All things considered, your husband is a very lucky man," the doctor reported at our meeting the next morning. The tumor was benign but had done a lot of damage. "We believe it had been growing for years, perhaps ten or more" he explained. "It's called a facial nerve neuroma because it actually strangled itself around the facial nerve and continued to make its way toward his ear.

It destroyed two of the three bones in his inner ear, which may leave him deaf, and grew toward the brain and actually tried to break through the dura, the brain's outermost of three layers of the meninges that's responsible for keeping in the cerebrospinal fluid. If the tumor had broken through, your husband would have been a vegetable. The spinal fluid would have escaped causing meningitis and no one would have been able to help him."

I could hardly believe what I was hearing. Joe had never complained of a twitch or twinge in his face, and here was the doctor, drawing pictures and showing me where and how this octopus-like tumor grew roots in all directions. Amazingly, Joe was one of only ten people in the country at the time with this type of tumor.

The doctor continued to explain that—because the tumor was so close to the brain—they had to leave a tiny piece of it so as not to cause further damage or paralysis to other parts of his body. Joe would suffer permanent facial paralysis and had lost his peripheral vision. He gave me instructions to watch carefully for any sign of escaping spinal fluid from either his nose or ears.

At 29, I possessed enough wisdom to know the road ahead would be difficult. Joe would have to retrain himself to drink from a cup without spilling it. A young, good looking man, he was vain enough to find his inability to wear contact lenses an adjustment for sure. I knew I had to find the strength to give to him so that everyday would be a gift to him.

Surely he'd be grateful that God spared him and he'd be around to see his babies grow up? When Joe got out of the car both girls ran to their daddy, so excited to see him! Tears welled up in my eyes as I watched.

Do You Love Me Because I'm Beautiful, or Am I Beautiful Because You Love Me…

Joe experienced great difficulty dealing with the way he thought he looked. He didn't want to look at himself in a mirror, and told me he'd never shave his beard once it grew in because he wanted to hide behind it. I tried to tell him beauty is within, we love you!

He reminded me how I felt—deep in the pit of my heart—when my doctor told us I had cancer of the cervix and a uterus filled with endometriosis. The possibility of not being able to conceive a child was traumatic for me. I knew my future was in the Lord's hands just like Joe's life today.

At one point I felt he might need counseling. After all, I had gone. I'd sought out help just before we met because I worried more about pleasing everyone then about myself. Through my counseling experience I learned that my parents controlling behavior was *their* issue, not mine. I couldn't make their past part of my future. I learned to forgive, to forget and to move on…to only take responsibility for that which I can control, and to let the rest go.

My greatest hope for Joe was that he'd come to understand what I had learned: that I must love and believe in myself in order to succeed. When you think positive thoughts then positive things can happen. He had to believe in himself; he had to keep the faith. If I hadn't freed myself of the weeds, I couldn't have planted my seeds and learned to love unconditionally.

The year after Joe returned to work he lost his job. We were barely getting on our feet and the portion of the hospital bill not covered by insurance totaled as much as a down payment on a house! That was when I made the decision we should think seriously about returning to New York closer to our families. What if Joe didn't recover and I wasn't able to work? We couldn't sell, so we rented our house and moved back north.

I enrolled in college to attain a master's degree and Joe started a new job. Not a month after settling in, my mother had both her breasts removed during one operation. I knew when her right breast was taken and my sister felt the left. Now hopefully cancer-free, Mom needed us back home, she needed my children—her grandchildren—to be there as motivation for her.

The doctor confirmed that he had sewn the back of Joe's ear at just about the time I'd felt the knife. He believed in mental telepathy too. And my mom's doctor confirmed that the time of her breast removal coincided with when I felt it happening. My love for my husband and my mother ran so very deep that my every breathe felt like part of them. God does things like that every so often and I don't question how or why.

I attained several master degrees from evening classes while working full time during the following years. Joe healed on the outside, but to this day I believe he is still trying to accept the way things are internally. My mom is a tower of strength who not only survived a double mastectomy, but also fought cancer of the colon several years later.

We stuck together as a family. Both Joe and mom share a vision: they say they were touched by the Lord. They witnessed seeing the angels. I say we are all touched by the Lord, and each of us—regardless of our paths—must stay focused on our future every day. We need to be grateful for the little things in life that we so often take for granted. Take it from me, the virtues of life are at your fingertips for the taking—and, like my dad says, "the best things in life are free…"

ABOUT THE AUTHOR: A veteran teacher for the Department of Education, Debbie teaches third grade in Staten Island, New York. She holds 3 Master Degrees - Special Education/Psychology, Administration and Supervision. For Debbie, teaching has always been a passion. Arrigo is a licensed Realtor Associate Broker in New York and New Jersey. Her outstanding ability to multi-task successfully and her strong work ethics has consistently earned top producer awards and personal recognition. As principle of a home based Travel Company, she has great presence within her community and business affiliates. Debbie is an advocate for American Cancer Society, March of Dimes and Autism Foundation.

Deborah Rae Arrigo
Educator & Entrepreneur
www.Debbiearrigo.com
ziadeedee@aol.com
646-235-4086

Tragedy Embraces Serenity

Karen Bomm

Exhausted, I opened my heavy eyes to see the sun piercing through my window shades as I rolled over on my living room couch to pick my ringing cell phone up off the table. I hadn't slept all night.

It was my paternal grandmother. Groggy from lack of sleep, I thought to myself: I don't *ever* remember receiving a call from grandma. Usually I call her before I make plans to drive over and visit.

"Did something happen, Karen?" I could hear the concern in my grandmother's voice.

"What do you mean, grandma?"

"I think something happened to Will." Will was my educated and successful father, her devoted son.

"How do you know?" I asked.

"I just feel something very bad has happened to him. I am very concerned."

"Well, I haven't heard anything, so there's nothing to worry about for now. Try to relax. I'll call you if I hear anything. Okay?"

"I am very concerned, Karen. Please call me if you hear anything."

"I will, Grandma. Thanks for calling."

I admired my grandmother's independence as a single German/Italian woman, now in her eighties. She had been the caretaker of my grandfather and her son, my father's brother, after they sold their farm.

Grandma lived in a wonderful retirement community that my father and my aunt (his sister) had affectionately and effectively set up for her. My grandfather died of Parkinson's disease well over a decade ago, and her other son, my uncle, had struggled with schizophrenia and died young of lung cancer.

I felt on edge but weak at the same time. My calendar showed no business appointments for the day, so, despite my grandmother's call, I rolled back onto my couch intending to focus on making up the sleep I'd lost the night before.

I wasn't sure what had kept me up all night, and why I'd received this strange call from my grandmother. My mind began to race, but finally my body relaxed enough to allow me to fall sleep again. I was awakened suddenly to my ringing cell phone. The call was from an unregistered phone number, and I answered it.

"May I speak to Karen Bomm?"

"This is Karen."

"Is your father Will Bomm?"

"Yes, why, who is this?"

"My name is Kevin Smith and I'm a nurse at Connecticut General Hospital. There's been a car accident."

Before he could even finish his sentence, I sat up on my couch wide awake now, and interrupted, "Did something happen to my father? Is he all right? What about my mom? Is she with him?"

My parents had been high school sweethearts. They'd been on their way to Martha's Vineyard to join my younger sister and her husband and their three kids on a family vacation.

"I'm calling to inform you that your father was just admitted into our hospital and is currently in intensive care."

"*Intensive care?* Where's my mother? What happened?"

Kevin kept our call focused on a discussion about my father's condition, which was serious, and refused to acknowledge or answer my questions about my mother.

I persisted until finally he told me, "Your mother was never admitted into the hospital." I froze, then went completely numb. I couldn't think, I couldn't feel, and suddenly the world was silenced by my scream.

My Accident

Ten years before I'd felt like my life was in alignment. I had my own radio show on which I interviewed holistic practitioners, and three mortgages, and everything seemed to be humming along nicely.

Then, out of the blue, as I made my way home from work one day, some guy with no license plates slammed into the right side of the back of my car. It was a rainy day, and I'd been turning a corner, so he clipped my car at an angle that threw my neck into a weird alignment.

Several months passed before I realized the severity of the impact of the accident on my body. All my neck and shoulder muscles cramped up as my muscle system started to break down. Aware that holistic treatments would best serve my healing purpose, I resented the main stream medical community's attitude. I wanted my treatment to consist of massage therapy and chiropractic care, but my insurance company wouldn't cover these modalities.

Pain became my constant companion…I woke up day after day in such unbelievable pain, it was never-ending, Ironically, it was this prolonged chronic pain—what I now call my "Dark night of the Soul"— that helped me face my fears and my own fate, and propelled me into a huge phase of awakening. During this period, my belief system shifted 360 degrees, and I evolved into a connected way of living.

My spiritual journey came through my physical pain, rather than through any mental processing. I focused on getting through the physical pain, which is what opened the door to integrating spirituality into my life. Always gifted athletically, this was the first time I decided to trust myself about my body, and not listen to what anyone else said.

I rejected the doctor's suggestions to do more damage to myself through recommended operations and procedures. I accepted that the body has much more intelligence than man ever does. This was about *my* truth; this was my journey. If I do it my way and believe in my true power and higher purpose/consciousness that it can be done, it will be done…

Through pain I experienced an intense mental free fall that forced me to break down all of the beliefs that were not serving me in order to reconstruct organically, from my soul up. Through the ensuing months I never got depressed, I always went into that third eye; that coach, that "you can do this." It was only when the physical pain took over that I went into the victim mentally. Then I'd pull out and say "oh, come on, you're not a victim!"

The Tragic Accident

In that one moment, my scream transformed from one of shock into one filled with the assurance that my mother had felt no pain. Her nurturing energy presence flashed into my living room and concentrated its center directly in front of me. It felt like a bucket of water that wasn't wet…it washed over and gifted me a sense of overwhelming peace.

Intuitively I knew my mother's spirit… she had come to communicate. She had graduated. I unconsciously felt like I connected to her on another plane of existence that confirmed she had instantly become part of something bigger than our physical world. She was okay, she was complete.

I envisioned liberating angels ripping away the chains that bound her soul. Grateful, I had no regrets, I understood she was okay and had simply moved on. She demonstrated the flow of life from one form to another in her transformation…in my transformation of observation.

My mother's warm energy kept me present though everything I'd experienced seemed surreal. I know she guided me through this shock, and gave me the strength to gather my thoughts about how to communicate this tragedy to my brothers and sisters, and eventually to my father when I arrived at his hospital bed.

My mother understood; she knew my dad was still alive. And I knew it was not my father's time to go, as he still had a reason to be here. He still needed time to embrace his peace and gift me the opportunity to ensure he knows how GRATEFUL I am for his presence as my father.

My mother's passing represented a birth in another form. Her death required me to have the courage to let go of something familiar–a breast, a hug, a kiss, a hand. My mother's peace in the midst of her tragedy gave me the strength to let go of all certainties, to rely on only one thing: my own internal power and connection, purpose & completeness.

Death and birth are essentially aspects of one process–LIFE. My mother's instant ascension symbolized transformation in its raw form. In some strange way, it was liberating to know she was at peace as she passed. She eloquently reflected a continuous flow of life from one form to another, and she transformed everything she'd touched and all to which she'd given birth.

(God) Grant me the serenity to accept the things I cannot change, the courage to change the things I can, and the wisdom to know the difference. (~Serenity Prayer)

ABOUT THE AUTHOR: Karen's mission to "create global wealth & health through communication, using simple tools that result in synergistic duplication," developed into reality after 12 years on Wall Street as an executive recruiter. Karen attracts TEAMS of "like minded leaders" to apply her ability to simplify complex situations into a "common sense conversation." Her shift to a more creative, intuitive, and organic business process involves the key component of "listening" as a way of thinking, doing and being. Karen utilizes her vision and inspiration to help others integrate awareness, be present, and connect to all aspects of life, both personal and professional.

Karen Bomm
www.LivingFreeSource.com
LivingFreeSource@gmail.com
720-982-4798

From Poverty to Possibility

Jordan Brown

"You were born with wings, why prefer to crawl through life?"—
Rumi

At the ripe old age of eighteen, I desperately wanted more in my life
than my one square-mile working class town. So I answered an
advertisement to be an aerobics instructor in an affluent neighborhood.
At that time, although athletic, the only aerobics I knew were Jane
Fonda's videos.

When the woman who interviewed me asked, "can you come in and
teach a class on Friday?" I trembled inside but said, "of course!" In two
days, after watching every possible exercise show in the middle of the
night, I created my own dance tape. I then drove my battered ten year-
old car— praying I had enough gas—thirty minutes to the spa.

Sweating and filled with anxiety, I stepped into the fancy spa. I
prayed that no one could hear my heart pounding out of my chest, or see
my accidentally mismatched socks! I was hired despite the fact that my
music ended ten minutes too early, and I left the spa incredibly excited.

To this day, I marvel that this one opportunity opened the door to
countless new friendships, exciting experiences, travel, and wonderful
relationships. The confidence that came from knowing I could do
anything—or at least that I could try anything—was exhilarating!

I'll never forget an article I read by Oprah several years ago, where
she describes sitting on the back porch of her home in Mississippi
watching her grandmother hand-wash clothes in a bucket. As Oprah
gazed out at the sky, her grandmother yelled, "pay attention girl, you're
gonna be doing this someday!" Oprah didn't dare say a word to her

grandmother, but she said to herself, "no I'm not grandma, no I'm not." I understood her feelings...

Growing up poor in Paterson, New Jersey, to a black Puerto Rican father and a white Irish mother was no fairy tale. My father barely graduated from the fifth grade, and fled Puerto Rico at thirteen after one last beating at the hands of his abusive mother. My mother graduated from high school with a one year-old child, and had four more before the age of twenty-five.

My parents worked incredibly hard, each holding down two jobs, and finally moved us out of poverty and into possibility, where they believed we had a better chance of success. I was taught never to say no to opportunities and to remain open to meeting new and different types of people. Over and over again my parents emphasized the importance of education, my own job, my own place, and my own money before I even considered settling down with someone. Forget being dependent on anyone—that was only in the movies.

Even though my parents expected me to achieve more than they did, and I knew they wanted me to be happy along the way, they didn't always have the tools to show me how.

It was lonely at times not having parents to walk me through college applications, registrations, and new apartments, but their support remained a constant. I remember when I told my mother I'd be applying to Columbia University School of Social Work in New York City, how she broke out in hives and said "why push it?" She never wanted her children to face disappointment. She knew it all too well and therefore didn't always believe so much was possible.

My father, learning of my plans for Columbia, bragged to everyone he knew that I was going to school in another country. He was elated when he later learned the school was New York. Never a dull moment with my parents! Always, their love shaped the course of my life.

Eventually, I finished school, fell in love, got married, moved to the suburbs and had a child. In time, we desperately wanted another child and, after years of trying to get pregnant, my health began to suffer. I despised my well-paying job, and when my husband was relocated to St. Louis for an entire year, I fell into despair.

One night, crying on the phone to my best friend, I sobbed, "are there people who love their jobs, have perfect families and don't have to spend their life savings on infertility treatments?" There was dead silence on the phone until he said calmly, "lose the job." I did not respond because I knew the truth. Holding on to something I didn't want was preventing me from having what I did want.

One cold, snowy, Tuesday evening I was sitting at my desk, wishing I was home, when the phone rang. It was my babysitter who frantically told me that my daughter had fallen down the stairs. Catherine was crying and bruised but not badly hurt. My heart sank—I was over an hour away, and that was without traffic. I will never forget that drive home because I knew I would not return.

Early Wednesday morning I resigned by telephone, effective immediately, with no job lined up and no idea what was next. I knew after I hung up that something had shifted within me. I felt physically different. I felt relieved, alive, and open to what lay ahead.

I picked up my daughter from school, excitedly told her I didn't have to work, and we headed to my mother's for dinner. On the way, my cell phone rang, and what I heard caused me to pull my car to the side of the road. It was the social worker from the adoption agency where we'd applied several months before.

"Your son was born," he told me. "You have a beautiful baby boy. Come tomorrow at noon and pick him up." It was 4:30 p.m. Overwhelmed, I felt like I was dreaming. Hysterical, I told him, "I just quit my job this morning and now I have a son?"

"Go shopping," he responded. "It's been a while since you had a newborn." I never asked a single question about the baby. I just knew he was meant to be my son.

As promised, at noon, we picked up our son and brought him home to share with the world. Truly one of the happiest days of my life, I was astonished how the week's events unfolded. I almost forgot the following day was my last infertility treatment.

Proudly, I brought my new baby to the medical center. The place had begun to feel like my second home. The warm and loving nurses hugged and congratulated me and the room was full with excitement. The doctor laughed and asked if I was sure I wanted to continue with the last treatment. I said I was ready. Not scared, not anxious, simply ready.

Two weeks later, I learned I was pregnant, and nine months later my daughter was born. Having two babies in one year was definitely a challenge. I knew I could not—and would not—go back to work at a job I hated.

Instead, I wanted to be present for my family and keep myself fulfilled and happy at the same time. I wondered if it was possible, and when I began to meet people who helped make that happen, who allowed me to learn everything I possibly could, I knew it wasn't just a pipe dream.

Soon I began to visualize my next move. I wrote affirmations, expressed more gratitude, and felt more confident about my choices. I surrounded myself with positive and encouraging people. I once heard a life coach speak at a seminar who said "you are the average of the five people you hang around." I laughed but totally understood. Always raise the bar. It's possible.

Although my dad died before I opened my own psychotherapy practice in 2007, his presence, acceptance, and love remain steadfast reminders in all I do. My mom, who passed away recently, watched my business grow and said lovingly "I am so incredibly proud of you and all you have accomplished—but please make sure the kids eat and your kitchen floor is clean."

Perhaps fairy tales really do come true…

ABOUT THE AUTHOR: Jordan Brown is a Psychotherapist, Coach and owner of Full Circle Counseling. She runs an In-Home Intensive Therapy Program for families in crisis throughout New Jersey. Jordan is a Board Member of The Holistic Mentorship Network and a columnist for M.A.R.C.I. Magazine on Conscious Parenting. Her secondary business, Jordan Brown Inspires, is the foundation of her work in Women's Empowerment, writing and motivational speaking. Her fire burns full-throttle, ignited by the passion she embodies and the drive to help others create the life they desire. Jordan is an adoptive, biological and step-parent to five children and lives with her husband Jeff in NJ.

Jordan Brown
Full Circle Counseling
www.fullcirclecounseling.net
Jordan Brown Inspires
www.jordanbrowninspires.com

Treasure Hunt

Sarah Carkner

As I lay in bed, swollen-bellied, helpless, and pregnant past my due date, I wondered when my drunken husband would finally arrive home. Anxiety twisted inside me like knots, as I prayed he would get home in decent enough shape to drive me to the hospital.

As fate would have it, an hour after he passed out in bed beside me, my water broke. In all my girl-hood fantasies, I never once pictured my Prince Charming drunk. So how did I end up marrying a man with a drinking problem? I don't even drink, for crying out loud!

Ours was a whirlwind courtship, during which drinking was never an issue. We socialized, ate at the best restaurants, and traveled—it was a carefree time for us both. Sure, when my husband went out with the guys he would have a few beers, but drinking was not a part of our daily life together.

It wasn't until the everyday challenges of marriage and the responsibility of preparing for a child set in, that I discovered my husband found his primary coping mechanism in a bottle. I naively hoped his excessive drinking would stop after our daughter was born. I wished he would look into her sweet, beautiful, trusting baby blues and feel compelled to deal with his issues.

Unfortunately, in the weeks following our daughter's birth the discord between us grew stronger. I felt like we spoke two different languages but neither of us had a dictionary to translate.

Between my raging post-partum hormones and our increasingly dysfunctional marriage, I frequently found myself in a daze. As I pushed my daughter's stroller through the park watching other seemingly blissful families, I'd think, "where did I go wrong?" and "how did this happen to me?" I found myself wishing I had my own happy family.

But problems can't be healed by wishful thinking alone. I didn't want to walk around in slow motion while the rest of the world continued to move full speed ahead.

I consulted a therapist who told me that if I divorced my husband, I needed to be able to look into my daughter's eyes and tell her that I'd tried everything I could to make the marriage work. This struck a chord with me, so I approached my husband and insisted on couples' therapy.

Although he obliged, I waited and waited to see any actual changes in his behavior. It was like watching molasses drip from a jar. For me it simply wasn't fast enough. I began to realize you can't push someone up a ladder unless they are willing to climb. I wanted to scream, "The ladder is right there! Why won't you climb?"

I felt totally depleted. I felt like a failure. I wondered what was wrong with me. I didn't like the way my husband preferred going to a bar over spending time with me, and I certainly didn't like having to walk on egg shells for fear that something I said would send him into a tirade.

Upset with myself for allowing another person, especially my husband, to treat me so poorly, I vowed not to put up with his behavior next time! But after an emotional apology on his part, the next time came and went.

I became someone I didn't recognize…someone I wasn't proud of. My marriage was sucking my soul dry and I began to feel physically unwell. But as one foot planted itself outside the door looking for relief, the other staked its claim inside, rooted there by fear of the unknown.

Suddenly I realized that—although I was fighting with my husband on the outside—I was actually at war with myself internally. The supportive wife sparred with the feminist in me on a daily basis.

I could choose to work on my marriage, but at what cost to my personal power and integrity? There seemed to be a fine line between the two, and it was on this line that I wavered.

While I value loyalty, commitment, and family, I equally value respect, trust, and communication—all of which this relationship now lacked. Most of all, I hated being in limbo with no clear direction in sight.

The Line in the Sand

And then it came. The line in the sand was drawn for me. I don't remember what our fight was about. It was so insignificant to me. Thinking our argument had ended, I began to vacuum the family room floor. Suddenly and seemingly out of nowhere, my husband aggressively grabbed me and moved me across the room.

Completely taken aback, I looked up at him in surprise. Immediately I saw that he was beyond angry. Our eyes locked, and that's when I saw out of the corner of my eye his raised fist. Though instinct should have told me to protect myself, I couldn't look away. Instead, I met his angry eyes with mine, and said defiantly "go ahead, hit me."

I don't know what caused the shift in him but, just as quickly as he'd raised it; he let his fist fall to his side and walked away. We both knew it was over. He left that day for his hometown, and I began putting our divorce into motion.

A week later my husband returned.

He got down on his knees, took my hand in his, and offered to buy my daughter and me a place to live—on our own. He acknowledged he had "issues," and told me sincerely that he hoped to earn his way back into our lives one day.

I'd expected his usual apology—which I'd already resolved not to accept—so his offer caught me off guard. Surprised, but relieved, I thought: *maybe we aren't done yet.* But still I doubted. "Did hell just freeze over?" I wondered, and "am I being punk'd?"

Awkwardness filled the car the day I agreed to search for a new home, one in which our daughter and I would live without him. We'd decided to make the best of the situation and see what happened. For curiosities sake, we followed a particular "for sale" sign, and we stumbled into what I can only describe as my dream home!

But it was a home for a whole family, not for a mother and daughter. As we drove away, I told myself that it was one dream I'd have to let go.

A few days later my husband called, promised to go back to therapy and to devote himself consciously and whole-heartedly to working on his issues. Then, after telling me he realized it would be a leap of faith on my part, he asked if I'd consider buying that dream house and living in it together, as a family.

I was stunned. I looked up to the sky and asked "God, are you pulling my leg?" Had my husband really turned a corner? Was he truly ready to climb the ladder? If so, was *I* willing to take that leap of faith?

Buried Treasure

It was time to look into the mirror of deep dark truth. Just as gold miners sift through dirt and rubble to reveal gold, I knew I had to sift through my thoughts and emotions to reveal my truth. I needed to wash away my hurt, my disappointment, my defenses, and all the blame that had built itself up around my marriage. When I got to my core, I knew I needed to take the path with a heart; I knew I had to choose love.

How could I turn my back on a man so willing to try to better himself? I believe in personal growth, in self-realization, and in practicing what I preach. I couldn't turn away from all the possibility and potential that lay ahead.

I also knew that I needed to make some serious changes in order to move forward. I decided to take the leap of faith, but this time I'd have both feet in the door. I realized I needed to focus on myself, and to emotionally release my husband to find his own truth in his own way. As I began to explore my wants and needs for an emotionally rich and abundant life—regardless of the current state of my marriage—I gained strength and tapped into my personal power.

And I knew I needed to forgive—both my husband and myself. I had wasted so much energy focusing only on his behavior. As soon as I let go of the notion that I could "help" him if he'd only listen to me, things began to change for the better. I stopped trying to "fix" *his* issues, and started to tend to *my own* wounds.

I turned my focus from trying to change the situation by changing him, to altering my perceptions of the situation. I began to read books on spirituality, attend lectures, create vision boards, and attend support groups. In short, I put into practice the very things I learned as a professional life coach in order to help my clients.

As my consciousness expanded, I experienced an awakening. The more I learned about my spiritual world, the more I realized I didn't know. And as I transformed from thinking of myself as a failure to understanding there is no such thing as failure, I began to see the light.

I became energized by the notion that there are experiences, and then there are my reactions to them, and that's it...I went from being ashamed of my marriage to being so proud of the effort we made to give our daughter the best of both of us.

Now I truly understand that you cannot put a period where God has placed a comma. Facing the challenges presented by difficult people and difficult situations can unearth one's "buried treasure" in the form of hidden talents, insights, and self-determination.

I am not going to lie, since my leap of faith, some days my foot makes its way for the door, and other days I look at my husband and think I actually see Prince Charming.

While each day is a journey, I now know that my renewed sense of self will grant me serenity and strength, and keep me moving forward no matter what the future holds… and THAT is priceless.

ABOUT THE AUTHOR: Sarah Carkner obtained her Bachelors in Neuroscience and Masters of Wellness Management while also pursuing her love of dance and fitness. An advocate of personal growth and self-development, Sarah acquired a Professional Coaching Certification and started a successful life and business coaching practice out of Malvern, Pa. Sarah has established herself as a local fitness expert and teaches exercise and dance classes to crowds of hundreds. No stranger to the stage, Sarah has appeared as a guest expert on "Navigating Your Life with Nat Williams," and presented at multiple venues, including Mind, Body, and Spirit Expo, and the Children's Hospital of Philadelphia.

Sarah Carkner
www.sarahcarkner.com
info@sarahcarkner.com
610-220-0393

All the Love in the World
Mary Caruso

The neurologist's voice on the phone was strained. My daughter's tests were back and the results were "worrisome," she said. "Come in tomorrow and we'll discuss it." My heart sank.

The next day as I sat across from her at her desk, I twisted my hands in my lap as I waited to hear the news. I trembled as she handed me a piece of paper with the words "Friedreich's ataxia—progressive neuromuscular disease" written on it.

I stared at her. I didn't know what it meant. But what I was beginning suspect with certainty was that those words meant that life as I'd known it was over. In one instant, without warning, all the hopes and dreams for my daughter disappeared.

What next? I barely remember the barrage of words that came at me that day by the numerous specialists who paraded into the room to talk to me. But I do remember the look on the face of the neurologist as she said—no doubt meaning to be kind—"take all your family vacations now, because you don't know how much time you have."

Later I learned that Friedreich's ataxia was so rare that the doctors didn't know what to tell me. No one knew what gene abnormality caused it, and they certainly couldn't offer even the slightest assurance that there would ever be a cure.

What I could expect, they said, was that Sam, my beautiful, athletic, feisty eight year-old daughter, would experience a progressive deterioration of all her motor skills, as well as problems with her heart, speech, and coordination. Eventually she would live fulltime in a wheelchair.

It was unbearable. I stumbled out of the hospital in shock. How would I ever explain this to my daughter? And even more importantly, how would I make her life as normal as possible, and ensure that she'd have all the fun and exciting experiences that I'd imagined for her?

When the shock wore off, I found myself reeling from the need to do something, anything, to keep from passively accepting what was happening. I sprang into action. If the doctors and scientists were unsure what to expect for people with Friedreich's ataxia, maybe I could help them find out.

I was no scientist. I was simply a mom, an art major, who recently achieved my dream of opening my own clothing store for children. It was a comfortable, warm, friendly store, where friends came by to shop and hang out and spend hours there with their children. My own two kids, Sam and her five year-old sister Alex loved being at work with me.

But now I bought a computer and spent hours searching anyone or anything that might be connected to this disease. I learned it was so rare that only a few people in the country were even researching it, and there was no organized effort to conquer it. I ran into one dead end after another. But finally, while searching online, I found other families— though only a few of them—who faced the same future for their loved ones.

Fate seemed to be at work in my life as I discovered, connected with, and befriended some amazing people who eventually became like family to me and my girls. As we bonded, this small group slowly became an organization.

Over the next few years, we met with health officials and government agencies, and over time spearheaded a successful research alliance that brought together international researchers, and made the first strides to find a cure for the disease. That successful alliance continues today.

It would have been enough of a life lesson for me to learn firsthand the power of a community, of connection, and to watch as our group raised enough money to fund scientific research and clinical trials for those affected by Friedreich's ataxia.

But life had even more lessons in store. Three years later, just as everything was settling down, Alex, then eight, was diagnosed with the same disease. The chances of that happening were one in four, but to me, it seemed impossible that another daughter would be claimed by this disease.

Unfortunately, Alex's bout with Friedreich's ataxia proved more severe than Sam's. My younger daughter, who'd told me from the time she was little that she wanted to be a dancer, became wheelchair-bound much sooner. She's also had more cardiac symptoms and undergone several extensive surgeries.

Now, fifteen years after that initial diagnosis, our lives are nothing like I'd ever expected when I was growing up and dreaming of having children. But neither are they what I'd been led to expect on that dark day when I first read the words "Friedreich's ataxia" on that piece of paper.

My daughters and I live together in a house that is wheelchair-accessible and we travel in a van that accommodates two wheelchairs. While both girls are limited in their mobility, they have succeeded in college and performed well in the working world.

Sam's degree is in film editing, and Alex has studied social work. It's true they have challenges with their speech and motor control, and that they must depend on others for assistance with the most routine daily tasks such as bathroom visits, showers, cooking, getting in and out of bed. But they have friends, are committed to helping other people, and are among the most compassionate, loving people I've ever met.

Human beings, I've decided, can adjust to almost anything if they really put their minds to it. While from the outside our lives must look completely surreal to families with healthy children, what we experience is normal to us. It's a life filled with laughter and love amid the day-to-day ups and downs: the emergency room visits, middle of the night health scares, and the constant erosion of the girls' abilities and coordination.

Here's the truth about a progressive disease: just as you get accustomed to a new limitation, something else happens. The progress of this disease can be cruel and unrelenting. And yet the lives we lead are magically close and loving, as we've found ways to cope together.

Maybe the truth of life is this: when you live with uncertainty every day, you figure out fast that you really don't have any control. I'll always be proud of the fact that our research alliance has helped scientists make such great strides toward a cure, even though that cure, when it comes, will be too late to help my own children.

But what I do know now—that I didn't know at the beginning—is that when you realize you can't control everything that happens to you, you're left with a genuine compassion for all people, and sheer, unbridled love.

What's left is appreciation for the moment in which you are living, and an urgency to be kind and loving to all of those you meet. That human connection is key to survival.

Don't get me wrong. I've struggled to change things, and railed against the fate that brought this into my daughters' lives. And if I could wave a magic wand and change everything, I would.

Tonight, as I write this, it's a typical scene at my house. The girls both have friends visiting. Sam and her best friend are watching a video on the computer and laughing at the antics of some rock group. Alex, who is recuperating from back surgery, is feeling well enough to eat a grilled cheese sandwich, and her therapy dog is angling for a bite, which is making my niece Mandy laugh.

It's a cold winter night and, as a friend stops by to drop off a banana cream pie "just because," someone else is bringing in some pellets for the wood stove. There is a lot of laughter at our house—laughter and commotion and chaos, the ups and downs of family life; long, deep talks, friendship, tears, wishes and stories. It's a house that seems to be always brimming with life.

Three weeks ago, the night before Alex's surgery, she awoke at four in the morning, lying alone in the darkness. I heard her quiet sniffles and went into her room. She was scared, she told me. What was going to happen? Would she be in a lot of pain? Was it all going to be all right?

I don't know quite how to put what happened next, the way it felt like such a privilege to lie there with her and just listen and hold her, and to say again the words that I have always told my girls: "None of us know what's going to happen next in our lives. Nobody has that certainty. But here is something I can promise you: whatever happens, we will go through this together. We have always gotten through, and we will continue to get through, because we have everything important to survive—we have all the love in the world that we need."

ABOUT THE AUTHOR: Mary Caruso studied at Paier School of Art and Southern CT State University. For fourteen years she had the pleasure of running a retail boutique and hopes that at some point in the future she will return to that. She is a "Kindness Activist" - instilling its importance to others in hopes of making the world a nicer and gentler place. Most importantly, however, is her role as life facilitator for her two daughters, her heroes, who travel through life with Friedreich's ataxia.

Mary Caruso
www.openyourheart-marycaruso.info
meirbode@aol.com
203-889-6484

No Small Thing

Sheri Horn Hasan

Ten weeks pregnant, I lay on the table where I'd undergone a routine sonogram to check on my baby's progress when the doctor solemnly informed me that the baby's heartbeat was no more.

Shocked and numb, I listened to his kind but clinical voice telling me that the baby more than likely had chromosomal damage and that the miscarriage was, in the end, for the best. As my brain consciously registered his words, my heart pounded and then silently broke. I was 41, trying to have the second child my husband and I had always wanted.

What I didn't know then is how this tragedy would trigger a series of life-altering events and propel me on my own personal journey of deep woundedness—one that would change the course of my life forever.

Six weeks following the loss of my baby I began to experience symptoms of intermittent tingling that ran from my right hip down into my thigh. Walking became difficult, and my legs felt like they weighed a ton as I struggled up and down stairs to chase after my extremely active pre-schooler.

Fatigued, and feeling worse every day, I visited my general practitioner father-in-law, who gave me a shot of cortisone in the hip. Several weeks later, when that proved ineffective, he x-rayed my hip.

The x-ray showed nothing unusual. Perplexed about my other symptoms—which now included vertigo, dizziness and the feeling that I had an imaginary belt cinched one notch too tight around my waist—he sent me to a neurologist for further testing.

All the while, the numbness continued to spread from my right leg and foot to my left foot, and continued to creep slowly up my left leg until it finally reached my waist. I marveled at how it seemed to "jump" from one side to the other, while at the same time I panicked about why.

The dizziness became pervasive, the burning pain in my right hip and thigh more acute, and walking seemed a mystifyingly demanding task. Such was my condition when, after examining me, the neurologist sent me for MRIs of the back and brain.

When I returned to him, MRI films in hand, he immediately suggested admitting me to the hospital where in all honesty I was quite happy to agree to go. Exhausted, confused, and dizzy, at least I'll get a reprieve from the demands of being a wife and mother, and an uninterrupted night's sleep, I thought.

Three MRI's, one spinal tap, five intravenous infusions of a high dose steroid later, and the diagnosis was conclusive: Relapsing Remitting Multiple Sclerosis.

The Wheelchair

MS is a chronic, progressive, neurological disease of the central nervous system, or the brain and spinal cord. It is an autoimmune disease in which certain white blood cells in the body, mistakenly thinking there is a foreign invader, attack the myelin, or the fatty coating that surrounds the nerves.

Myelin enables the nerves to transmit electric impulses from the brain throughout the body. When the myelin is attacked and eaten away by these rampaging white blood cells, nerve conduction is impeded and the result is tingling, numbness and intermittent loss of feeling in whatever particular area of the body the attacked nerves traverse.

After pronouncing his verdict, the doctor made it clear that if we wanted another child, and I relapsed during my pregnancy, there would be no relief. My other choices were to forgo another pregnancy and begin taking one of the injectible medications to try to slow the progression of the disease. Or I could do nothing and take my chances.

And he was fearful I might relapse quickly—within only three to four months.

To make matters worse, my doctor father-in-law, in an attempt to be helpful, told my husband that if things did not go well for me I might end up in a wheelchair sometime within the next ten years.

I struggled to cope with this momentous news. In the months that followed, the realities of this disease were tough at first to digest. It was even tougher to believe that I would at some point fully recover the feeling in my lower body and be able to walk normally and take care of my now five-year-old son without succumbing to total exhaustion.

And then I woke up one morning, still exhausted, partially numb, and intermittently dizzy—still terrified and depressed about my future—when something inside suddenly clicked. This is *my* life and not my disease's, I reasoned. How could I live the rest of my life in fear? What kind of existence would that prove to be? Was I really going to just accept that I might be in a wheelchair one day and have no control over my own destiny?

I recognized early on that I could choose to take to my bed, pull the covers over my head, and refuse to face each day. Or I could put one foot in front of the other (no small feat at this point) and go as far as I could—*one step at a time.*

The image of Scarlett O'Hara in *Gone With the Wind* kept coming to mind. The climactic scene—just before the intermission—where, having returned to her father's decimated farm she finds him feeble and confused.

She realizes that it's all up to her—she alone must keep the family alive. As she digs desperately in the dirt in search of food, she triumphantly finds a carrot. Raising it high up to the sky she declares: "With God as my witness, I'll *never* go hungry again!"

I knew I could never just give myself over to this disease. I resolved early on that—whatever MS ultimately had in store for me—it would not *beat me.* I vowed, "with God as my witness, I'll never *not walk* again!"

With that realization, I determined to live *my* life *my* way. And I understood that the definition of *"my way"* could be *whatever I wanted it to be.* I decided I had to live my life, make my plans and if, in the end, I woke up unable to carry them out, I would deal with it as it came.

I resolved to learn as much as possible about MS. I joined the National MS Society's mailing list, attended a local support group, went to patient programs, and read everything I could get my hands on about the disease.

I lay to rest the goal of a long-desired second child, and understood that it was not in my cards. My doctor suggested I go on a particular

immunomodulatory drug therapy he believed would take effect quickly—
he was fearful I might relapse sooner rather than later. I argued with him,
saying I wanted the one with no side effects. I didn't care if I had to take
a shot each day. I refused to give in.

As I began taking the daily injectible drug that *might* help slow the
progression of the disease if it proved to work for me, I returned to the
study of astrology, an area of great interest in my earlier days. The
astrological philosophy that events in our lives may be fated, but that we
are all born with the freedom to *choose* our own paths to our ultimate
destinies, intrigued me. I realized that life is *always* a matter of choice!
And I was choosing to look at my glass as half full, rather than half
empty.

Waking the Personal Will

In time, I began to realize that a lot of my "issues" had to do with my
inability to express myself. I was daddy's little girl, but looking back it
seemed that I always had to chase him for attention. When he'd smile at
me and call me "cookie," I'd light up like a Christmas tree! It took the
experience of my MS diagnosis and going deep through my astrological
study to realize how tyrannical he'd been when I was growing up.

Did he abuse me? Absolutely not...but was it his way or the highway?
Hell, yeah! So I came of age subconsciously "stuffing" everything I feared
to express. And that's how I eventually got diagnosed with an
autoimmune disease in which the body attacks itself...hoo boy, did I
really need THAT big of a wake-up call?

It didn't take too long after that to make the leap to my husband and
my marriage. Controlling and angry, he prevented me from expressing
my personal will over and over again. At first, I was willing to
"compromise," but when our son was born, his behavior became
increasingly controlling. I'd retreated and avoided, for the sake of peace.

A year after my diagnosis, most of my symptoms decreased
substantially and I no longer had to take to my bed by 7:30 p.m. each
night when my husband returned from work. When my first post-
diagnostic MRI of the brain showed no progression I was ecstatic! My
first call was to the pharmaceutical rep for the maker of my chosen
medication, with whom I had struck up an acquaintance. She was as
excited as I about my positive results.

Shortly after that call, she invited me to become a patient advocate. When she explained that I could share my experience with others newly diagnosed with MS, I jumped at the opportunity. What a blessing to be able to speak with others who faced the same terror and uncertainty in the early days of their diagnosis as me, and to reassure them that they had choices, as MS was by no means the end of their road.

Two and a half years later, my health improved to the point where people did not believe I had MS. I initiated a divorce, continued my study of archetypal/psychological astrology, found full-time employment as the marketing manager with a non-profit organization, and refused to live my life in fear of what tomorrow might bring.

Most importantly—now that eleven years have passed since my diagnosis—I *never* experienced the relapse predicted by my diagnosing neurologist. I know that I defied the odds. I continue now with my volunteer work as an MS patient advocate, practice as a professional astrologer, and have swapped a full-time job for my own writing/marketing business.

While I pray for a cure for MS, I count my blessings and hope that ongoing MS research one day finds a cure, so that when I picture my future, it does not contain a wheelchair.

And believe me—that is no small thing.

ABOUT THE AUTHOR: Sheri combines her twenty-plus years experience as a writer, editor, and marketer, with her intuitive ability to bring other's ideas to life on the page. Her promotional writing business *Sheri Gets The Word Out!* expresses your message clearly, accurately and concisely, expands your exposure, and inspires your audience to understand intuitively through the beauty of the written word. Also a professional astrologer, Sheri applies her knowledge of archetypal and psychological astrology and her intuitive capability to help bring clarity and direction to the lives of others through her Karmic Evolution Astrology business. She continues her life-long mission as a patient advocate for multiple sclerosis.

Sheri Horn Hasan
www.SheriGetsTheWordOut.com
Sheri@SheriGetsTheWordOut.com
www.KarmicEvolution.com ~ 732-547-0852

Only This Love
Bonita Kline

"How do you keep this going when you return to the real world?" The question came from a lovely young woman who glowed from her recent "awakening," just having experienced a newfound connection with her inner power, or life source, at the retreat I was attending.

I'd returned to this retreat—one I'd assisted teaching many times—to open and relax, to just be present. I'd been living spiritually awake for a number of years and was curious to observe this beginning event, where many people experience "awakening" with fresh eyes.

The young woman continued, "For example, how do you react when you meet a woman with an ugly baby? I know you can't actually say it's ugly, but from this space of truth, how do you handle this?"

My mind drifted back to a time when my perspective on the world around me was transformed in a most powerful way.

We had come to the Children's Museum to see Maurice Sendak's Chicken Soup with Rice exhibit, and the boys quickly found their way to the noise making room. My five year old and bubbly toddler were laughing and enjoying the music room when I noticed a young mom and her toddler had joined us.

The toddler laughed and banged on the musical pipes, then suddenly turned to look at his mom. It was then I noticed that a lump the size of a tangerine protruded from his forehead. Despite his beautiful face and smile, it was impossible to avoid noticing this abnormality.

The young mom stayed focused on her child and did not see me. At first I wanted to ask her about it, and to offer support, but I knew I'd be interfering. Suddenly, I surprised myself and quickly ushered my boys into the next "fun" room.

I didn't remove them to protect them from something I considered abnormal. At this point in their short lives, they'd seen all kinds of "abnormal," including beggars on the subway and homeless people on the street—which for kids growing up in the city doesn't seem strange at all.

Rather, I feared what my boys might say. My parents told this story of my older sister at age three. While the family sat eating in a restaurant my sister noticed an armless man eating with his feet.

"Look at that man eating with his feet!" she'd screamed, as the whole restaurant full of people turned to look not only at the man, but at my sister and my parents as well. Overwhelmingly embarrassed, my mother never forgot the humiliation.

So I ushered my kids away, fearing one of them would scream out something that would embarrass all of us, especially the woman and her son. I paused to look back at them as I left the room, hoping to offer a smile of understanding. They were laughing and playing, and did not even notice me. Always empathetic, I struggled with the pain this young woman must be going through. For months afterwards, I worried about the child and wondered if he was alright.

My Turn

Eighteen months later I would think of them over and over. After pre-school one day my son's eyes had crossed and he couldn't walk straight. A trip to the emergency room, followed by a day full of tests, and my little Christopher was diagnosed with an inoperable brain tumor. Within days he lost the ability to walk. His eyes crossed and his neurological function diminished daily.

As word of Christopher's condition spread, people began to visit us. It was a comfort to have people around to talk with, to console us. And though their intentions were good many did not realize how hurtful their comments could be. "I wanted to see him while I still can," said one friend, and "we wanted to play with him before things get too tough," said another.

Some well meaning friends took lots of pictures of him, believing they were doing me a favor by indicating they'd provide me with lots of photos by which to remember him.

I tried to explain that we had lots of pictures of him already. We took a lot of pictures as a family. Dealing with his prognosis was hard enough, and these well meaning friends only thrust more daggers into my heart. This was *not* how I wanted to remember my son, *if* he did actually die. At that point, I completely stopped taking pictures of all three boys.

Chrissy gradually lost all function in his body and limbs with the exception of two fingers on one hand. Even his facial expressions changed as the tumor paralyzed half of his face. He no longer looked like my beautiful boy.

We carried him from room to room and helped him get comfortable on the pillows while he observed our family activity; participating in any way he could. We'd bring toys to him, and help him play, read books, make up stories with his toys, help him manipulate remote control things, whatever we could do to make his day happy.

One afternoon, while we had visitors, his two year old brother started pulling his clothes off one arm in dramatic arrangements and parading around for everyone to see. I'd worked in the fashion industry my whole life and was quite amused by his runway performance, as were our guests.

As my little one continued to rearrange his clothing and create a new look—now knowing he was entertaining us all—I struggled with my decision not to take pictures of my children at this time. Knowing my younger son needed the attention; I hesitantly grabbed my camera and snapped some photos of my little stylist.

When the excitement calmed down I heard Christopher call for me. When I got there he said quietly, "You can take my picture, Mommy. I'll smile really big for you, Mommy. A really good smile."

"Of course I will Chrissy," was all I could say. As I turned to get my camera, I quickly wiped away my tears before he could see them.

Guilt, shame, anxiety, fear, and pain all ran through my body as I walked down the hall. He must have noticed I'd stopped taking pictures. Did I hurt him by not wanting to have a permanent reminder of him sick?

I wanted to take pictures everyday with my kids. I wanted to laugh and cry and run and jump and play with them. I wanted more outings, more days, *more life.* Dear God, he was only three years old. I wanted a miracle. I wanted the tumor to go away. I wanted to get back to our normal lives and take normal pictures of our beautiful, healthy children again. It was so unfair. Tumors happened to old people, not healthy, growing children.

There is a special kind of love involved in taking your child's picture and then looking at the pictures later, together. You let them know you love them so much and that you want to remember them always. If my boy could walk and talk and play he would have been right in the middle of the scene, clowning around with his brother.

His desire to be normal was so strong, but at the same time he didn't seem to mind what was going on with his body. He was patiently waiting for the doctors to make him all better. He was patiently waiting for me to take his picture, with love, like normal.

When I walked back into the room, he was working really hard on smiling for me. I tucked the sheet neatly around him and stepped back to snap the photo. He looked up at me with one eye, the other focused in a different direction. He smiled with half a smile, the other side of his mouth frozen because the tumor pressed on the nerves.

I saw in my son's face a gentle glow. "I'll smile for you, mommy." His face was filed with love. All he wanted was to love and be loved in return. Like any child. Nothing else mattered; only this love.

My son died about a year later. I never saw the well-meaning friends' pictures and I am glad for that. I have only this one picture of Chrissy at that time, along with Alex's fashion poses. When I first saw it after he died it made me cry. But my pain was not grief. It was guilt-guilt over my judgment that my son always had to be beautiful and perfect.

In time I learned to forgive myself. I realize these were my feelings, not his. He didn't see himself as deformed, just waiting to get better. He did not see himself as less loveable, and he wasn't.

I look at that photo now and see that glow, that really big precious smile, just for me. I see the love.

I never knew what happened to the young mother and little boy from the museum. I pray that whatever abnormality they were dealing with disappeared and they are now living joyful, healthy lives.

So, what *do* you say to a mom who has a baby that is not quite beautiful? Each of us has to look inside and answer that question from our own space. For me, there are no ugly children. There are only children who want to love and to be loved in return.

My young Christopher was my greatest teacher. He reminded me that day that he was still my beautiful child, no matter what. This was the first of many things he would teach me during the eighteen months of his tumor journey.

He taught me what unconditional love truly means. When we live in unconditional love, we "see" that which our eyes cannot. We perceive beauty where others may not. Only through this love can we feel the power and freedom that is already within us.

ABOUT THE AUTHOR: Certified as a Visionary Leadership Coach, an Accredited Journey Practitioner and a Reiki Master/Teacher, Bonita draws on her 25 years of leadership experience in the fashion, textiles and theatrical industries to inspire others through team, group, and individual coaching. The success of The Business Clarity Workshop Series© for small business owners, created by Bonita with input from colleagues at Freedom Within, "stems from the depth and quality of the process work we bring into partnership with our clients," Bonita explains. Bonita is a founding partner in the Conscious Leadership Coaching Partnership, an international initiative aimed at serving businesses and organizations on a global level.

Bonita Kline, Founder
The Kline Boys Fund
www.TheKlineBoysFund.org
Partner, Freedom Within, LLC
www.FreedomWithin.co
freedomwithinllc@yahoo.com

In The Moment

Barbara Maida

It is two days before Halloween in Bensonhurst Brooklyn, 1959. Matt the vegetable man is planted in the midst of his stand's colorful fall vegetables and waves hello as I walk past. I love this time of year.

I live in a small apartment with my mother, since my dad left a few months ago after he confessed to having an affair with the waitress at our family-owned restaurant. My mother is angry at first, and I help her move all his clothes to my grandmother's apartment next door. I'm glad he's gone. All he ever did was drink and yell. I never felt he loved me.

Now, as I walk home from school at the age of 15, I am sad for my mother. She is hurt and lonely, and I wonder how I can make her feel better. I run up the three flights of stairs, happy to be home. At the door of the apartment, I stop suddenly. What is this? The milk bottles are still outside our door.

My mother would never leave them there all day, something must be wrong. I enter the apartment, feeling frightened. It is dark and quiet—I go into the bedroom and she is in bed, her face in the pillow, the covers drawn up to her neck.

How can this be—my mother never sleeps late, and it's four o'clock in the afternoon. I walk over to the bed to wake her but she is hard as stone. Oh my God, terror sets in. In a daze, I walk around the bed to the phone and call my grandmother's house.

My uncle answers. "Help!" I scream into the phone, "I can't wake up my mother!

He runs over and turns her over in the bed. Who is that, she is like a stone statue, her hands in fists next to her face. That face, who is it, stone cold white, its mouth open, fangs showing—who is that?

My uncle calls for help, I stumble into the living room, grab onto the credenza to hold myself up. I sit on the couch—I cannot think, I cannot feel, I am numb all over. People come through, the police, my grandmother, so hysterical. The police tell her to get it under control and take care of me, but she never does.

My father comes, crying Helen, forgive me, but it's too late.

Finally, my Italian landlord and her daughter come in and take me down to their apartment, where they give me a shot of whiskey. But I am still numb, this is a dream, it must be, this cannot be real.

My friend and her mother arrive; they take me home with them. We sleep three girls together in a bed. I am grateful for the warmth of their bodies.

Funeral arrangements and confusion, where will I live, I cannot go back to that apartment! I am grateful for the funeral, this woman in the coffin is my mother, but will I ever forget that grotesque statue in her bed?

At first I do not cry. When they close the coffin, I know I will never see her again. Suddenly my heart shatters into a thousand pieces, and I cry so hard the priest comes down from the altar to console me.

Then it is over. It is decided I will live with my grandmother, uncle and father in their apartment.

I am alone, my uncle and grandmother never speak to me except to tell me what to do. My father is not there at all; he's at his restaurant all night, drinking after closing, sleeping while I am at school and gone when I get home.

I know I need to take care of myself. I pray and pray, go to church, ask God why me, but do not get any answers. I am angry at God, at my mother for leaving me.

Everything is a nightmare, I dream of my mother being alive, only to wake up in this hell hole of a life. She loved me—no one else does. I do not fit in at school or with my friends. I am sad and alone. I shut down. I vow that nothing will hurt me again—I am tough and strong, and I will survive.

My Three Angels

I swear that I will never marry a man like my father, but guess what, I do.

We marry, the perfect couple, two beautiful people, the perfect family, two beautiful children. His career is very successful; we have a big house, a lot of money, and on the surface look perfectly happy.

After 16 years of marriage he leaves and we begin a divorce.

I always thought that my mother's death was the worst thing that could happen to me. Nothing else could possibly be as traumatic, I figured. But I was wrong.

The first year of my separation I thought I would die. I was 39—the same age my mother was when she died. I did not think I could physically or emotionally survive the destruction of my family. The thought of watching my children suffer killed me, but there was no alternative. If I left this world, I would leave them alone with this man, just like my mother did to me.

Once again, I survived. I found help in the form of a nutritionist who helped heal my body, and a women's center that offered a support group for divorced and separated women. Immediately after that, I found my angels.

My first angel was my lawyer. A new lawyer working for a well known divorce firm, he was young, handsome, and aggressive. The minute I met him, I knew he had the strength to take on my husband, and he did.

My second angel appeared just before my divorce trial when a friend dragged me to a singles sailing club party. Little did I know that I would meet a retired school teacher and sailor, who would change my life! Fifteen years older than me, he was kind and never raised his voice. He actually spoke to me; cared about what I had to say, and proved to me I was a woman.

After years of being told I was cold and not affectionate enough, I discovered that I loved sex and dancing and sailing out on the ocean. Sitting on that boat as it floated upon the water was like being back in the womb. God had sent me another angel to begin my healing.

Later on, I knew I still needed to heal. I declined the invitation to move to Florida with my new male companion, who was ready to retire.

I decided instead to move into the city and start a four year psychotherapy and healing program, determined to heal no matter what it takes.

At this point, I wonder if I'm ever going to be free to be me. And who is *me* anyway? I have been a daughter, a mother, and a wife—but who am I really? And why do I continue to suffer?

In this program, my third angel appears in the guise of a psychotherapist named Art from California who embarks on the mission of teaching a group of us body work. For the next three years we do workshops in body-oriented psychotherapy about four times a year, including an annual retreat in California.

I learn that before I can work on the anger I feel for my ex-husband, I need to work on the anger I have for my father. I learn that I need to find myself and be present in the moment before I can heal the past.

Art begins our workshops by reminding me to be present. I think to myself: what is he talking about—I *am* present, I *am* here! But I was not. Over the course of time, I learn how much I dissociate, or leave my body as soon as something painful comes up.

I remember listening to someone in our group talk about her trauma (discussion was a regular part of our learning/teaching sessions), and Art saying "Barbara stay with us, stay present," and I realized that I had just zoned out. I didn't want to hear her painful experience, so I did what came naturally to me—I dissociated.

Through my private sessions with Art I work on what I now identify as trauma that began when I discovered my mother dead in her bed that day in Bensonhurst.

Art asked me to go to church every day and receive communion. At first I resisted the idea, but I went anyway. Little by little I began to find solace in this practice. I'm not even sure I prayed, but attending mass and receiving communion provided some comfort, and I began to believe that maybe this time God would hear me.

When the workshops ended I still did not feel healed. So I went to California to spend a week working with Art.

It was there that a miracle happened. Normally during our sessions I cried my way through the retelling of the trauma of finding my mother that day. But this time I suddenly stopped crying—all of a sudden it was as if a curtain came over me, and I experienced a strong sense of closure.

Confused, I actually felt strange and different in my body. I felt elated, oh my God, I actually felt alive! I was shocked.

"What happened?" I asked Art.

"You've healed your trauma!" he explained.

"What now?" I asked.

"Now, your life will be different," he answered. And he was right! I had finally learned how to be present in the moment.

Next, he introduced me to his Buddhist teacher Tenzin Wangyal Rinpoche, and I began to learn the Bon Tibetan Meditation practices that I still follow today.

It was through these practices that I discovered a true spiritual aspect to my life, and reinforced the notion that it's not about changing past or future events, it's about how you handle them *in the moment*.

ABOUT THE AUTHOR: Barbara Maida has spent the past 20 years exploring the relationship of food to health. While studying nutrition and holistic health she realized the connection of emotions and the impact they have on our health. She began studying psychology, hands on energy work, and herbal remedies to improve the emotional health of our bodies. For the past fifteen years she has been relaying all she has learned to her clients, working with them to establish what is best for them and then working closely with them to achieve their goals, through, nutrition, psychotherapy, body work, meditation and prayer.

Barbara Maida
Whole Body Awareness
www.wholebodyawareness.com
BarbMaida@aol.com
718-285-4942

The Divine Spirit
A Story of Triumph
Alisa L. Oglesby

It seems like only yesterday that my perfectly healthy, independent, sixty-two year-old mother called to tell me "I have to see an oncologist/hematologist in the next few days." It was December 2007 and, although miles apart, we spoke daily, she from her home in sunny South Florida. We were in the midst of finalizing her plans for her annual Christmas Holiday visit to South Jersey and she'd waited until the end of our conversation before she broke the news.

I immediately went into protective mode—I knew I had to remain centered and grounded for my mother's sake. I remember telling her that whatever happened we would go through it together. I can still hear her sigh of relief as she replied, "Yes, yes, I know we will…"

The following morning, after only three hours or so of broken sleep, I awoke hoping it had all been a bad dream. However, I knew I wasn't dreaming. I felt sick and wanted to stay in bed, but my business partner and I had an important meeting that day about a new office location for our home healthcare agency.

A few days later my mother went to the oncologist. I wanted so badly to stop everything and fly to Ft. Lauderdale. But I couldn't; I had scheduled meetings with potential referral sources for my agency. So I went the scheduled meetings and put on the best face possible, but all the while my mind was on my mother—was she afraid, how was she doing, what would she find out? I felt guilty, but consoled myself with the knowledge that she'd be here with me and my family within a few weeks.

I could hardly hold back the excitement as I drove to the airport to pick up my mother. We embraced; she had lost weight but looked good. She'd undergone a battery of tests and we'd decided to wait to review the results until after the holidays, and to face any potential health challenge in the New Year. We decided not to worry, since her health care providers had my contact information in case they needed to reach my mother during the holidays. During her visit she stayed in bed more than usual, ate less, and skipped our annual trip to New York.

We finally mustered the courage to listen to the message from her physician on New Year's Day. We rejoiced upon finding out it was not leukemia! Our theme: "Everything's Great in 2008!" A few days later she returned to Ft. Lauderdale and to her active lifestyle.

Or so I thought. My calls to her increased steadily, from one, to three, and even four times per day. I noticed she was becoming less active and that she'd missed several of her normal meetings. This was totally out of character for her. Three weeks later, I decided to make the trip to Ft. Lauderdale to "see about my mother."

At this point in my career, I'd made numerous presentations on both baby-boomer issues and the "sandwich" generation. I could hear myself saying to my audiences: "You call your aging and/or ill parent and ask how they are doing. Your parent tells you 'I'm fine,' because he or she doesn't want you to worry. What they don't tell you is that they haven't gotten out of bed in a few days, haven't eaten, and are not well." I then always ask my audience, what does "fine" look like?

I knew I had to see for myself. I rushed to my mother's condo upon landing in Ft. Lauderdale. My routine had always been to call my mother and let her know I'd arrived safely. Then I'd immediately visit my favorite restaurant and shops. This visit was different; I had to see my mother.

What a change in such a short period of time! I fought back my tears as I recognized immediately that my mother had lost additional weight, and seemed to have aged well beyond her sixty-two years. I could see the relief in her eyes; her "only child" was now by her side. I knew intuitively we needed each other and the universe was confirming divine order. My one week stay turned into six weeks. After more tests and doctor visits, we finally received a definitive diagnosis.

We quickly decided the best solution was for my mother to receive treatment at Fox Chase Cancer Institute in Philadelphia, only an hour's drive from my home in New Jersey. That way she'd get the best treatment, wouldn't be alone, and I could be her patient advocate and caregiver. In addition, I could continue to tend to my own business and grow my home care agency. It was March when we arrived in South Jersey for her temporary stay.

Perfect, Whole and Complete

In the midst of two operations, follow-up visits, scans, ultra sounds, and blood level checks, I remember my mother asking me what she should tell her friends. "Tell them you're perfect, whole, and complete," I replied simply.

In early December 2008, we got the best news since the journey began. My mother had progressed very well, and did not have to return to the doctor for two months. We were very happy; she returned home and called her friends and family to share the good news. We decided to spend Christmas and the New Year in Florida, since she had endured so much cold weather already in the north.

When we arrived in Ft. Lauderdale mid-December with the great news, we agreed this visit would be a trial run for her living independently again. Up and about early each morning, she was happy to prepare her condominium for the holidays. And she was excited about seeing her twin brother, his family, her friends, and her church family. She was doing fine and had looked forward to returning home. After all, she could return to the South Jersey for treatment as needed.

Shortly after, my mother and I attended a grief workshop at her church. A reception followed the workshop, and many people greeted her one by one, and told her how good she looked and how her she'd been missed by her church family.

The next morning she told me that she wasn't feeling well, but was determined to go to church and serve as a greeter. Her social calendar was filled with lunch invitations from many of her closest friends.

On Christmas Day, she was not feeling well again, but wanted to have dinner with her twin brother, sister in-law and family. Over the next several days, I monitored her closely and consistently, asking "do you need to go to the hospital, are you in pain, etc?" She assured me, she was "alright."

However, on December 31, 2008 the universe had a higher plan. My beloved mother became an Angel. I remember, standing at her bedside for over seven hours in the ICU, rubbing and thanking her lovingly as she transitioned. I reflected on our theme, "Everything Is Great in 2008."

Looking back now, I am forever grateful that I was blessed to spend the last year of her life together. We celebrated Mother's Day, both our birthdays, and took short trips; I felt my commitment to support her through her illness allowed us to enjoy truly meaningful time together. In addition, I knew that she'd gotten to see her friends in New Jersey, and that she'd managed to returned home to her church, friends, family and beloved twin brother.

A New Beginning

Within weeks of my mother's funeral, I returned home to discover my husband's infidelity and business collusion with his girlfriend. I filed for divorce after twelve years of marriage, and rather than dwell on any seeming losses, I chose instead to welcome the opportunity to mediate and move on.

It has often been said that death and divorce are two of the most emotionally draining occurrences in life. My mother's presence is with me always. I perceive her around me as she leads me into right actions, protects me from deceit, and comforts me during times of doubt. In the midst of my shock and emotional turmoil, I can clearly feel the many blessings flowing from her.

I embraced my "new reality" to create a higher dimension of purposeful living by starting another company, consulting and sharing my story to educate, motivate, inspire, and empower women to realize we have strength beyond measure and that there is good in ALL situations.

I am now taking the first steps in my journey towards my newly envisioned empowerment workshop conference series for women and children.   As I reinvent myself and develop my "spiritual brand," I continually pursue options that will elevate me to purposeful living at this phase of my journey. Every day, I say "yes!" to spirit and I rest assured that the universe is directing me to my higher good…

ABOUT THE AUTHOR: Alisa L. Oglesby's motto "Embrace the Journey, Enjoy the Ride, Let Spirit be your Guide," emerged from her own spiritual journey of transformation. A spiritual entrepreneur, motivational speaker, consultant, and author, Alisa is the president of OMG Women United, LLC, and ALO Women United, LLC, organizations dedicated to motivate, empower and inspire women experiencing loss to reach within and let their "Best Journey Begin". Alisa also applies her 25 years in sales, marketing, customer service and business development with Fortune 100 companies in the automotive, insurance and pharmaceutical industries to a homecare agency in southern New Jersey of which she is the co-founder/owner.

Alisa L. Oglesby
OMG Women United, LLC
www.omgwomenunited.com
info@omgwomenunited.com

Courage To Stand

Mikita Orosz

On that dark day—Black Monday, I now call it—while my husband prepared to leave for a business trip, the children and I were in the midst of our usual Monday morning scramble: lunch boxes ready, faces washed, and me crouched under our kitchen table lacing Pokemon sneakers as they enjoyed oatmeal and played.

We'd just returned from a ski trip in Colorado and our bags, still bulging with woolen sweaters and coats, sat waiting in our foyer to be unpacked. It felt good to be back home. Little did I know then that it would be months before the sweaters found their way back inside our closets.

I heard my husband call me from the master bathroom. He stood facing the mirror, knotting his red corporate tie. As I approached him, he turned around and said, "I want a divorce." His tone was matter-of-fact, as if he was telling me, "this is a new tie."

A stay-at-home mom with three sons and a daughter, I was a multi-tasking dynamo by day and a stalled whirlwind by night. He too was a multi-tasking dynamo, a successful CEO of a large company who shuttled around the country in his corporate jet.

Black Monday marked the first time either of us uttered the word *divorce*. Divorce happens to other couples—not to us. Fifty percent of marriages end in divorce, but not mine.

His announcement hit me like the news of a loved one dying from a common cold—traumatic, yet absurd! No one dies from a simple runny nose! Good marriages don't end in divorce! Yes, we had problems—small, repairable obstacles. But divorce?

And what about our children? And our dreams? What about me? Our children were eight, eight, six and four. I suddenly felt old at forty-one.

We'd been together all of my adult life. We were college sweethearts at NYU and our life together was straightforward and carefree. He is of Scandinavian descent; I come from generations of Asians and Spaniards. Petite, pretty and perky met strong, sweet, and sexy. We didn't own a car back then. Once in awhile he treated me to a ride around campus on his mountain bike. I'd sit balanced on the handlebars, while he weaved through Washington Square Park along cobblestoned side streets with the bustle of the city at our backs, and the power and innocence of youth in our hearts.

Twenty years later and we had amassed five cars, a fishing boat, a sunfish sailboat, eight bikes, several scooters and a big red wagon. Life got complicated.

He moved out, and Black Monday lingered on. It discolored Tuesday and Wednesday, and then April and May on through February. The biggest mystery was why? *Why* was he destroying our incredible family? I deserved answers. We deserved to work things out.

His decision was final. All he offered was, "I'm not happy being married to you."

I spiraled into a deep jagged crack in the earth, shoved into the crack by my dearest friend and partner. On the surface my life shone bright and wonderful— healthy family, big house, ski place out west, beach house up north, good friends, sound investments, no debt.

My Constant Companions

Lonely in the dark, I found new friends. My "crack buddies," *Self-Pity*, *Fear*, *Blame*, and *Rejection*.

My friend, *Blame*, focused on my attacker: "It's your husband's fault! He deceived and betrayed you!" He pretended things were okay for twenty years. He never mentioned being unhappy, and now he shares his discontent, builds a wall between us, and insists that it's too late to salvage our marriage. I feel there is no time limit on fighting for our family, and I'm frustrated that he can't hear me through the impenetrable wall!

My other friend, *Denial*, accused him of having a midlife crisis and pointed out the obvious: he's reliving his twenties, cruising on his new motorcycle, and hanging with a young bottle-blonde bimbo! And what's with the pre-ripped, low cut designer jeans? What happened to the old familiar faded Levis? *Denial* diagnosed: He doesn't have marital issues. He has inner struggle, personal development issues. He'll snap out of it.

I waited for him to change his mind, certain his intuition would spark an epiphany and guide him back to me.

I recalled our annual ski trips. He'd always lead the way through the snow, carving a sinuous path for our family to trace. Our children glided close behind while I brought up the rear shooting photographs. My husband challenged our children to go faster while I trailed behind recording their triumphs, always ready to scoop them up should they fall. We had a perfect system for everything.

For six months after his announcement, I drove only where my children needed to go. I hated bumping into acquaintances, especially those compelled to recount having seen my husband on a date.

The 24-hour Wal-Mart became a godsend. Two a.m. to four a.m. were ideal hours to shop. Half the time I never entered the store, I sat in my parked car and cried.

I cried daily. When my children caught me sobbing, I lied, "It's my childhood friend, Lisa, dying of cancer." I couldn't divulge that divorce had spread through me like a mind/body/soul-sucking disease.

I reminisced about the past, how my husband often came home to cheers and hilarity as the children and I played hiding games to make us all laugh. We'd hear the garage door open and they'd scatter to hide behind couches, under tables, and in the pantry. I'd shout our signal, "I don't know where they are!" On cue, my husband entered the kitchen asking, "Where are the kids?" Unable to contain their excitement, the children leapt from their hiding spots, screaming as they raced to tackle their father to the floor. Our home was a constant patter of eight happy, little feet.

One day, I managed to grocery shop during daylight hours. As I scanned isle number one with my buddy, *Self-Pity*, I noticed products my husband liked—organic low-fat vanilla yogurt, baby Swiss cheese— ordinary reminders of the life I missed. *Self-Pity* keeps calling me a loser; I am not even good enough to buy him his groceries. I lost the courage to brave beyond the dairy isle. By the exit, I stepped on the scale and weighed in at eighty-seven pounds. His rejection wore me thin and ragged.

It hurt to breathe. When I inhaled, shards of glass pricked my lungs. I grew tired of feeling fragile. Weary of a broken spirit, I went into my children's bedrooms and softly kissed them on their lips. I took two beach towels—the thickest I could find—and jammed them on either side of the door leading to the garage. While my children slept next door, I sat in my car in the garage and contemplated suicide.

I phoned a friend in New Jersey. I was cold and trembling. She told me things I had long considered, like the horror of my children growing up without me. A year of sadness whittled me down to hopelessness. No hope, no joy, no respite. Tomorrow would be the same. I turned on the ignition, closed my eyes, and waited.

I dozed off and hallucinated that the toxic fumes had somehow drifted past the jammed towels and poisoned my children. Thoughts of my cowardice suffocating them jolted me out of my crazy death wish. I can't believe I let it go this far!

"In life we cannot avoid change, we cannot avoid loss. Freedom and happiness are found in the flexibility and ease with which we move through change". ~ Buddhist teaching

In the year following, I opened my heart to the wisdom of spiritual leaders and healers. At sunrise, I'd sit on my bedroom floor and meditate with His Holiness the 14th Dalai Lama. Meditation allowed me to be in the moment; it removed me from the drama of my past and future. Guilt held me stuck to a past I couldn't amend, and worry kept me fearful of future events I couldn't control. "Who needs the drama?" Dalai Lama asked.

The pains in my chest gradually disappeared. Finally, I understood my body's plea to breath differently, to live differently.

Miguel Ruiz and Mohandas Gandhi tucked me in at night as they enlightened me with stories about acceptance, forgiveness and unconditional love. I learned to accept that I would never understand the reason for my divorce. I forgave my husband for knocking me down and then I forgave myself for keeping me down.

I learned that happiness eluded me as long as I was inflexible to the changes in my life. The more I resisted reality, the longer I suffered. I had waited for my husband to change his mind when all along I had to change mine. Sometimes it takes more strength to just let go than to keep holding on.

The negative voices in my head subsided; I stopped believing in their lies. When fear and rejection insisted I wasn't good enough, I challenged their message. Were my fears based on truths or limiting beliefs? Am I really not good enough?

The truth is, I've always been good enough, worthy enough, strong enough. The truth is, I've always had the choice to be unstuck.

The wave of choice and change is exhilarating! I can't wear blinders as I surf the wave! I ride balanced and fully engaged, no longer living in automatic mode. I bend with the undulating flow of life.

A white Salvation Army truck crossed my path the other day. On the doors read "Doing the Most Good" and "Working with you to repair broken lives." My heart filled with gratitude as I thought about my private army of salvation—my spiritual leaders and my children. They are the compassionate denizens in my soul who gave me courage to stand.

Today, my former husband and I share an amicable relationship and continue to positively co-parent our children. We still manage to keep some old family dreams alive. I share my newfound courage as I work with families facing difficult changes in their lives. It is my professional and personal mission to empower others to rediscover their inner strength and truth. And every day, I express my gratitude by enjoying life.

Three years ago, I married a beautiful man, a kindred spirit. Our blended family is an inspiration of love and harmony.

ABOUT THE AUTHOR: Mikita is a certified life coach, facilitator, speaker, columnist on SportsLink Magazine, avid community volunteer, aspiring pro-photographer, and inspiring stay-at-home mom. Fueled by her desire to manifest optimism and positive energy, she co-founded HeartMindMatters, a relationship coaching company and LifeCoachSuperstore, a company that creates motivational products.

While HeartMindMatters allows her to empower clients in the areas of Separation/Divorce and Family Coaching, LifeCoachSuperstore challenges her artistic and entrepreneurial spirit. Prior to relationship coaching, Mikita spent 10 years as a top producer for a Wall Street executive search firm. She lives in Florida with her husband, four children, two stepchildren, dog, lizard and two frogs.

Mikita Orosz
HeartMindMatters
www.HeartMindMatters.com
mikita@heartmindmatters.com
954-384-6696

The Poetry of Life
LaNette Parker

I stood on the curb and watched as the blue minivan pulled around. It was Saturday afternoon, and while most mothers were retrieving their seventeen year-old daughters from the movie theaters, mine was picking me up at the hospital.

Several minutes before, I touched my cheek to my day-old infant daughter's. I kissed her forehead. I gently laid her down in the snowman outfit I'd purchased. I rubbed her belly. As I rubbed and listened to her breathe, I checked to be sure the note to her adoptive parents lay next to her in the bassinet.

I didn't say goodbye. The nurse turned her cart away from me and took her from the room. I stood alone in an empty room. The candy striper came and motioned me into the wheelchair.

On the highway home, my mom broke the silence. "Mom and Dad will never talk about this unless you bring it up." I didn't bring it up. Only a few close friends know. Megan is now 21. While I knew with certainty Megan was a gift to this world, I didn't trust that others would see it that way. I wanted to protect her.

I measured my years by her birthdays. By the time she was one, I had moved to the Midwest to college and a clean start. By the time Megan was six, exactly four of my close friends knew of her existence. When she was seven, I moved further, to the West Coast, and reunited with her birth father. It was not meant to be. By the time Megan turned ten, I'd begun my climb up the corporate ladder along with an unhealthy relationship that would last years.

I couldn't see in my mind's eye whether I had kissed her. The pain of that final moment, the ending of my unplanned pregnancy, didn't come back to me until my daughter's fourteenth year.

It was then that I opened my eyes. The relationship I was in was unraveling and some days I just wanted to scream, to tell everyone about Megan. I began to understand how much time I'd spent waiting…waiting for happiness to find me…waiting to see Megan again. Waiting for the happiest day of my life, that was so far in the future, it was a pipe dream.

When I realized this, the grief poured out of me in a wash of tears. Where was I to go from here? I wanted a happy life…and deep down, I wanted a family with children.

I began to share my experience more in the hopes that it would help others. I started to heal my relationship with my parents by talking about Megan. I wrote on a piece of paper exactly the type of man I wanted in my life—someone kind and loving and stronger than me. And I accepted that, if he didn't exist, I would be fine. I said "yes" to every invitation.

I Know Why the Caged Bird Sings

One day a friend offered me an extra ticket to hear Maya Angelou speak to an exclusive audience. Of her own teen pregnancy, Maya said, "children pass through us." This perspective reverberated through me— a mother's role is as a vessel to bring her child into the world.

That afternoon I met my future husband. Two weeks later I told him about Megan. He hugged me and through tears told me I was very lucky to have a daughter. Within months we were married.

By our fourth anniversary, we'd been blessed with two sons. I was ecstatic. Our family complete, I designed a mother's ring that included Megan's name. I put her picture alongside my sons and talked with them about her. I felt more confident, free to be myself. I earned my coaching credential and started working with others who searched for happiness.

I dreamed of the day I would leave my corporate job to devote myself to coaching, writing, speaking, "mom-ing." But road blocks popped up along the way. When my husband became one of millions liberated from his job, it seemed I'd be forced to work full time longer than we'd planned.

We held fast to our plan to move to a lower cost area and live as a close-knit family. But life seemed hard some days and all I could concentrate on was what I didn't have…and what I didn't have was "my turn!" When I dropped my kids off at day care, I'd ask myself why the universe gave me three children to give to others to raise. In my nightly talks with Spirit, I began to plead *when is it going to be my turn?*

After a particularly difficult and busy season at work, my husband and I decided it *would* finally be my turn. If we trimmed day care expenses, used our savings, and performed freelance work, we could make it. We *could* spend delicious years with our young children. I planned to talk to my boss about a transition. But first I took a pregnancy test to appease my husband, who felt that my complaints about my body were a sure sign I was pregnant. I kept protesting, "no way!"

But, sure enough, he was right. When I peed on the stick and saw the two blue lines, I bent over, sobbing. I watched my future crumble in front of my eyes. Why would the universe give me another child to pass over to a babysitter? I'd *never* be able to leave my job, now that I *really* needed the stability of a regular paycheck and health insurance.

The same dark fears that appeared during my unplanned pregnancy at seventeen washed over me that day and in the weeks to come. Embarrassment and humiliation engulfed me as I regressed into the guilt of being the "dirty girl" caught having sex.

"Why me?," I asked, as I assumed the role of victim yet again. At thirty-eight, I found myself begging the universe to "make this go away," but at the same time was guilt-stricken by the knowledge that so many other women would gladly trade lives with me. Terrified the baby would be a girl, I sank into my knot of emotions—how could I raise a daughter when I'd given another away?

Finally, I came face to face with my previously unspoken fear—that I simply wasn't "good enough." Not good enough to be a mother because "good" mothers didn't give their kids away and keep having more.

"Stop!" the higher part of my consciousness implored. What was I talking about? Wasn't my sons' laughter and singing proof every day that I'd produced happy, healthy children? And I saw Megan's kind heart, brilliant mind, and acceptance into one of the top schools in our country, through annual updates from the agency.

I began to see light. I released my tight grip on my "plan" and broadened my heart to include the possibility of raising three children, of being the mom of four. Secretly, I began to long for a daughter and to have her feminine energy surround me every day.

The Light from Within

My newfound glow quickly diminished when we learned that our baby possessed significant birth defects in utero and, if brought to term, wouldn't live a quality life. Through the fog of medical terminology, we also learned that our baby was a girl. Given the severity of her defects, my husband and I never questioned that our daughter belonged in Spirit and not with us. The night of the ultrasound, I lay in the dark and once again asked why I was being forced to give away my daughter.

Then I remembered Maya Angelou's words—"children pass through us"—and realized that, for whatever reason, my daughter had chosen *me* because I was a great mom. I possessed the strength to give her all my love during her short time, to let her go, and spread her message to others.

That night, I talked to her and explained that her brain hadn't developed properly and that she'd have no opportunity for a full and happy life. I told her that, as her mother, I needed to do the best thing for her, no matter how hard it was for me. Over and over, I said, "I love you." From the darkness, I heard a baby's voice twice respond, "Mommy."

By the next morning all movement in my belly stopped and my pregnancy symptoms quickly evaporated. No more kicking, no more cravings, lighter breasts, smaller belly. One of my best friends, a healer, laid her hands on me. During the healing, I let my mind float and chanted "I love you" to my daughter. The message changed to "I love me." I felt my strength as a mother, felt the "not good enough" melt away, saw the beauty and blessings of my circumstances.

Within days, I gave birth to Ava Divine. We chose birth so we could hold her close, smell her, see her. In her imperfection, she was beautiful and perfect.

In our last moments together, I touched my cheek to hers. I kissed her forehead. I gently laid her down in the "little sister" outfit my oldest son had chosen. I rubbed her belly.

As I rubbed, I knew she hadn't breathed even one breath. I checked to be sure "Mother," Maya Angelou's book of poetry, lay next to her in the bassinet to be cremated with her. I thanked her for all that she had given me. I told her I would see her again.

I walked out of the hospital, my strong and protective husband and my parents by my side, and breathed in the bright blue California sky. I felt complete. Then we climbed into our car and headed toward the ocean. On the way we spoke of Ava and life and what we had learned.

Epilogue

The lessons of Megan's and Ava's lives are simple, yet profound: Know that *you* matter and that judgment does *not*. Accept your strength and greatness. Believe in the impossible and lean into the love and beauty of the moment. And *always* remain open to the rarest of finds: an intelligent young woman with a generous heart, and a red-haired girl who winks at you knowingly.

When this wisdom passes through you, you will have met my daughters. As for my sweet sons, my four year-old recently shared, "Your boys are turning into a work of art." Indeed.

This is the poetry of life.

ABOUT THE AUTHOR: LaNette Parker, ACC, CEC, is an easy-to-talk-to credentialed coach and Motivation Factor® certified partner, who specializes in helping you visualize and achieve your happiest day *today*. She partners with you to help you overcome fear and circumstances, so you can fully experience joy in your life. In addition to her "character building" life experiences, she has many years in corporate human resources and communication consulting. Her favorite people are her spirited, fun-loving children, who don't let anything get in the way of living their happiest days. She is also a global collaborator on The Difference Project, an international movement aimed at opening humanity's heart.

LaNette Parker
www.lanetteparker.com
lanette@lanetteparker.com ∼ 415.317.3371

The Silent Voice

Carole Sacino

I remember four things clearly about the day my mom and I shared a special "girl's day out"— it was April, it was cold, it was magical, and I had the awful feeling that I might never see her again.

It was 1960, I was seven years old and headed the next day for open heart surgery at Children's Hospital in Boston.

After weeks in a coma, I awakened to find my mother at the end of the bed and my grandfather holding my hand. He welcomed me back with a smile as big as life itself.

Delighted and excited, I opened my mouth to speak, but to my surprise no sound came out! Turned out the operation had resulted in some kind of damage to my vocal cords. But the doctors said it would be temporary and told my parents not to worry.

However, weeks turned into months, and soon I was off to speech therapy to learn how to speak again. With four siblings—and only 11 months between each of us!—this limited raspy voice was quite a challenge. And the kids at school were not very forgiving. At first, long and lonely days provided me with a profound sense of abandonment.

Then one day, as I was sitting alone in my room, I suddenly heard a soft beautiful voice whisper to me: "You are a gift from God here on earth to help others—we are always with you." I felt a warm protective glow around me. Just the sound of the voice—never mind its message— gave me such an overwhelming feeling of love that I knew then and there I would never be "alone" and that I only needed to have faith in myself and everything would always be ok.

Excited, I shared my experience with my mom. But the look on her face shocked me. It was one of embarrassment mixed with pity. "Oh honey, don't be telling people that story!" she cautioned me.

Once again, at such a young and naïve age, I was silenced. I realize now in retrospect how unusual I was to verbalize my spirituality at that tender age, but at the same time how it was considered inappropriate to express myself in such a way. And so the message came through loud and clear: Stay silent and keep your "weird" thoughts to yourself! From that moment on, I learned to silence myself in the outside world. I gave up my power to others, resigned to the fact that I would not be heard.

Many times over the following years the little voice in my head held me back from jumping on the stage and taking a position…I let others speak for me time and time again. But inside I continued to believe in a higher power—one that always guided and protected me.

In fact, I felt bold enough to try lots of things even when the outside world told me I couldn't or shouldn't, or that I wasn't smart enough, strong enough, or worthy enough. I tested my teachers, friends, family, and the establishment, and continued to prove to others that I am not only here to survive, but to thrive in the face of adversity.

Of Those Who Say Nothing, Few are Silent

Meanwhile, it seemed that everything had to do with my voice. The connection between my inner world and the outer world—that should have been bridged by my ability to speak, communicate, and connect—remained weak as I struggled with my less than perfect ability to be heard.

Silencing myself completely was *not* an option, so I forced myself to learn new survival skills. Easy to hear in a quiet room, I nevertheless felt invisible wherever background noise existed. Where I could go and be heard drove my choices in life—where I could sit, who I could connect with, what I could and couldn't do all had to be contemplated before I made my move.

By the time I was old enough to frequent bars, clubs and restaurants, I never sat in the middle of the room. That was the worse spot for me! And forget about the middle of the dance floor…One night, out with my friends, this good looking blue eyed babe walked right up to me (yes me!) and asked me to dance!

Heads turn and—butterflies in my stomach—we headed to the dance floor. As he tried to connect with me by asking questions, I couldn't speak loudly enough for him to hear my answers. He quickly moved on to someone else for the next dance and I was left frustrated and disappointed.

Avoiding those I wasn't interested in talking to was the flip side of that coin. And believe me, I used it often enough! If strange guys hit on me, I only had to start talking and when they couldn't hear me they'd move on to someone else—great diplomatic way not to hurt their feelings! And still, I found myself smiling a lot just to feel included in the conversation. But I often felt judged by others.

Nevertheless, the bar scene proved fascinating to observe, and I loved watching people and trying to connect with them. I eventually decided I wanted to be a bartender—what a great job! So I went back to school. Not just any school—I went to Harvard! My dad was so proud to tell everyone his daughter graduated from Harvard.

Well, I graduated with honors from the Harvard Bartending Course "Art of Mixology" that prepared me to be a professional bartender. My dad would just leave out that little detail!

As soon as I got my certificate, I landed a job at a hot local bar. My first Saturday night (big tip night!) the bar was packed three deep and I had a blast keeping up with the drink orders, which came fast and furiously. But, unable to yell loudly enough to tell people how much they owed, I'd watch as they disappeared into the crowd. Then I'd have to chase after them to collect!

One time a group of girls ordered drinks and then walked away without paying. I tried to call out to them, but they kept walking and I had to pursue them into the crowd…"Hey, you owe me for the drinks," I tried to shout, but they just kept walking. I had to get up in their faces before they finally gave me the money. We almost brawled right there on the floor!

You Can Speak Well if Your Tongue Can Deliver the Message of Your Heart

Undaunted, I realized that I could accomplish anything I set out to do—it just took determination and perseverance, that's all… Several friends suggested I would be great at sales. I was shocked. How could I sell if I had difficulty being heard?

But the more I thought about it, the more the idea appealed to me. I am a people person and I love to communicate! I wasn't going to let my voice (or lack thereof!) hold me back…

My first opportunity was selling for a leading dictation equipment company (how ironic is that?) as a straight commissioned sales person. I would demonstrate how to use the equipment. When I excitedly told my parents about this big opportunity, my dad reacted incredulously. *"Sales? You don't have what it takes to be in sales!"*

Well, that was all I needed to hear! I challenged him to see who would make more money one year from that day. And out the door I went with the drive and determination to prove him wrong. One year to the day after, I went back to him to match pay checks and watched him eat his words!

Over time my successful track record led to many promotions. The voice of my dad ringing in my head, I made *my* voice my power tool in small intimate settings. But still I faced challenges as I moved up the corporate ranks, where it's not so much what you say but how you say it that gets you noticed.

Recently, and since my move out of corporate America and into my own business, I happened to watch a show on television with Dr. Oz called "Your Voice Could Be Killing You." The more I listened, the more emotional I became.

The show filled me with hope that there could actually be something physically wrong with my voice. What are the odds that—50 years after my heart surgery left me without the power of a strong voice—I should suddenly discover there might be a solution?

Immediately I decided to take action.

Within days I had an appointment with a leading ENT specialist who confirmed that I had a paralyzed vocal cord, likely the result of my surgery. There existed a relatively easy procedure to fix the problem, he assured me. Sign me up! Without hesitation and with hope in my heart, I went in for surgery. The operation was quick and recovery fairly easy, but no voice for the first week!

By week two—as I write this—my voice has begun to get a little stronger. I love wine tasting events and, in the past I would sip, spit, and smile, without communicating much in the loud environment. But for the first time at a recent tasting event, I was able to talk with others and be heard!

I watch the power of positive work its miracles every day through my own company, the Turning Point Institute. Here I focus on teaching others how to tap into personal power, passion and purpose through motivation, engagement and accountability. Through my work, I continue to learn not to silence the voice of that scared seven year old who just wants to feel safe.

This past year I also became a successful Alliance Partner with Motivation Factor® to help launch this amazing program into the United States. As a "connector" and one who builds strong relationships, I have to take the stage from time to time.

Now, instead of becoming frustrated and angry at missed the opportunities to speak for myself, I realize it's a new day! With offers to speak coming at me left and right, it's time for me to step into my personal power, claim my voice and say "yes!"

ABOUT THE AUTHOR: Carole Sacino, Principal of Turning Point Institute, a consulting company providing solutions when the goal is to Engage, Commit and Motivate individuals and teams toward a common purpose (objective) with results from the inside out! She has spent 20 plus years in the publishing/media industry in multiple sales and senior executive level leadership positions driving business and change. A strong passion and purpose for mentoring, coaching, discovering and developing the high potentials "athletes" in the industry with a specific focus on cultivating women leaders. Carole is a Certified Professional Coach, Master Practitioner in Energy Leadership and emotional Intelligence and Motivation Factor ® Alliance Partner.

Carole Sacino ~ www.turningpointinstitute.com ~ 617-299-1198

The Great Blue Heron
Dale Schock

My husband lay in the ICU, bloated with sixty pounds of extra fluid. His skin was stretched so tight it looked as though it could rip apart at any moment. As I tried my best to hold it together, inside I was scared to death that I might lose him. Hooked up to every machine imaginable, he was fighting desperately for his life.

He's too young to die, I kept thinking. Though I knew intellectually that we were all going to die one day, until this very moment I'd never thought about either of us actually *dying*. Glenn was only 58—I'd imagined we'd be together forever!

But at this moment, mortality stared me in the face.

Suddenly, I was startled by one of the monitors that began to beep loudly. Three nurses rushed into the room, pushed me out of the way, and commanded me to wait down the hall; they would call me.

I reminded myself of my belief in God and that He takes care of everything! When my daughters were born, I'd looked at each beautiful, perfect baby, with her ten little toes and ten little fingers, and knew that only a higher being could have created such wonders. I was in awe of these tiny miracles that God had entrusted to me.

As a little girl I'd feared death. I remember my recurring nightmare: I was with my family. I would die, and they would die, and then we'd all come back to the same family. The dream went on and on until it faded to black. I would wake up in a cold sweat, frightened and in tears. The nightmares stopped by the time I was a teen, and my worries about death seemed to dissipate. Since no one close to me had actually died, I guess I pushed any thoughts of death aside.

When my Mom passed away, I thought I'd made my peace with death. The night she died, *she* was at peace; her face glowed and she looked ten years younger. I knew she was in a better place at that moment, and that a wonderful life waited for us beyond this earthly existence. Perhaps, I reasoned, death isn't so bad after all.

But now, as I stood in the hallway and watched the nurses and doctors run in and out of Glenn's room, my fear of death resurfaced. I struggled to keep my composure as the loud beeps, sirens, and commotion continued for what seemed like hours. I had to be strong. I had to handle it, like I always handled everything that was put in front of me. But the tears just kept coming, rolling down my cheeks. I felt like a child again back in one of my nightmares! Would they be able to save him?

Finally they motioned me back into the room. Glenn was stable. I looked into his eyes and saw *his* fear too. I gently took his hand, and squeezed it to reassure him and remind him of what we always said to each other, "together we can do anything, nothing can touch us!"

The Symbol of Hope

When Glenn and I met more than forty years ago, it was love at first sight! Throughout our life when times got tough we pulled closer together and always came out on top. This would be no different, right?

Emotionally, physically and spiritually drained, but confident that he was stable, I left the ICU at three in the morning. All I remember about the ride home was how I'd gripped the steering wheel and cried out to God, why is this happening? I even yelled at my mom for not being there when I needed her so much…I felt broken and weak. How was I going to be able to handle this?

I sat at the kitchen table the next morning and stared out at the lake. I felt cold and empty as I tried to prepare myself mentally and emotionally to return to the hospital. Out of nowhere, a Great Blue Heron appeared.

The first time I'd discovered a Great Blue Heron sitting on our dock was the morning of my mother's passing. Family and friends came and went all day, but the Great Blue Heron remained, never moving. The next morning the heron was still there—it just sat and watched over us.

Since then, the Great Blue Heron always appears whenever there is a major event in my life, good or bad.

Seeing the heron now brought me tremendous comfort; it was as though Mom's spirit, my Guardian Angel, was present to give me the strength I needed. Even though I still hear my Mom's words in my head and feel her love in my heart, the Great Blue Heron always brings confirmation.

This morning I felt a powerful energy well up from within. My body started to warm up and the emptiness began to dissipate. A feeling of unconditional love surrounded me. I felt hopeful and strong.

Back to the hospital I went, not knowing what I would find, but knowing I'd be confident enough to handle it. Glenn looked much better, and he was hungry—a good sign. I felt my tension ease a bit. It would be a better day. Then came good news—he was doing so well they transferred him out of ICU.

The next day I waved to the heron as I left the house. When I arrived at the hospital, Glenn was just back from some tests. He looked stressed and his breathing was labored. I felt the dread creep in, but quickly pushed it away.

Two orderlies came in and transferred Glenn to a gurney to be taken for more tests. As they stepped outside the room, he started thrashing, suddenly unable to breathe. His lungs had filled with fluid and he was drowning. Trapped on the other side of the bed, I screamed for help. Somehow I got a surge of super-human strength, picked up the bed and, lunging for my husband, caught him before he fell to the floor.

I saw the sheer terror in Glenn's eyes, and I tried to calm and reassure him until the nurses finally arrived. The heat of anger rushed to my face; I couldn't help but feel that this wouldn't have happened if he was still in the ICU.

It became an endless night. They'd placed a mask over Glenn's face, and were forcing oxygen into his lungs to try to push the fluid out of them. I watched his every breath, movement, and the monitor for the slightest irregularity. My heart went out to my husband; he looked so terrified, fragile and tired.

I sat awake for what seemed like the longest night of my life. The machines would set off alarms, nurses would rush in, and Glenn would panic and rip the mask from his face. As the hours wore on, I knew it was up to me to take control.

This man was my partner in life; he'd always taken care of me. And now, it was my responsibility to make sure that he got well. I was committed to giving him everything it took—mentally, spiritually and physically. I had tunnel vision; he was going to live, even if it was through my own sheer force of will!

During his three weeks in the hospital, he grew stronger and stronger. Good thing, because he would have to be strong for what came next. The doctors informed us that his condition was due to kidney failure, and that he'd be forced to be on dialysis for the rest of his life.

The rest of his life, I thought. At least that meant he would live.

The Strength Within

In my days at the hospital I drew upon strength within me that I hadn't even known was there. Sure, I had dealt with some pretty tough times. I'd made it through my mothers' passing, devastating financial circumstances, rifts in the family, and my own health crisis. Somehow this was bigger than any of them. It felt insurmountable.

And yet, I found peace in taking action. I *could* do something about this. As Glenn started regular dialysis, I began our journey toward alternative treatment. I found healers, supplements, and modalities that improved his condition. On the internet day and night, I talked with friends and colleagues for hours, and did everything possible to keep this man in my life.

Now, as the days pass, Glenn and I find joy in the little things. Every morning, he greets me with "how's the love of my life today?" When he comes home from work or dialysis, I always stop what I'm doing to greet him and talk about his day. We have fun no matter what we're doing, even if it's grocery shopping. We're closer now than we've ever been.

Glenn's brush with death woke me up to life. I look at things differently now. I recognize that no one is immortal—not even me. I enjoy my dad and family more, and we're closer than ever. I feel more pride for my daughters, who've grown into beautiful and loving women.

I feel closer to those friends who have shared my sorrows and my triumphs.

Since then, I've learned the symbolism of the Great Blue Heron. Native American Indians believe that wisdom and good judgment are inherent in the Great Blue Heron. In Egypt the Heron is honored as the creator of light, while the Chinese say the Heron represents strength, purity, patience, and long life. And in Africa, the Heron was thought to communicate with the Gods.

Always a good omen, the Great Blue Heron also symbolizes the need to go with the flow and work with the elements of Mother Nature, rather than struggle against them. I now believe that this great bird's appearance on the day of my mother's death was her way of telling me—after all of her years of unconditional love—that I am more than capable of being able to trust my own innate wisdom as I maneuver my way through life...

I know we are surrounded by love. My mom makes sure of it.

ABOUT THE AUTHOR: Dale's many hats throughout the years include those of bookkeeper, bank teller, stay-at-home mom, networker, artist, caregiver and entrepreneur. While searching for a remedy for her own itchy, painful rashes, Dale joined numerous wellness companies from 1993-2003. Her passion was ignited when she discovered that many of the products she used contained toxic ingredients that caused her chemical sensitivity. This led to her current mission to educate consumers about how to find safer products and replace toxic ones with healthy, eco-friendly versions, and AlphaZelle was born! AlphaZelle offers healthy, eco-friendly, toxin-free (clean and green!) household products for the whole family, including pets.

Dale F. Schock
AlphaZelle LLC
www.alphazelle.com
dale@alphazelle.com
201-213-4178

PART THREE

Transformation
Through
Spiritual Awakening

*"What I am actually saying is that we need to be willing
to let our intuition guide us, and then be willing to follow that guidance
directly and fearlessly."*
~ Shakti Gawain

French Toast Freedom

Ginny Caroselli

I stood at the kitchen table in our apartment, dutifully slicing his French toast exactly the way he insisted it be done. He was in the shower preparing for work.

As I cut each piece of French toast, flashbacks of our entire relationship flooded into my brain. The same man who surprised me with an engagement ring in a fortune cookie later twisted my fingers and tried to break them.

The same man who'd written piles of love letters over the years also slapped and punched me hundreds of times. As the painful truth began to reveal itself, I fell into despair knowing I would never be able to please him.

I recalled the sound of shattering glass when he attempted to push me through a second floor window. I remembered how my panic and terror escalated as he held me over a bridge and threatened to release me into the raging waterfalls below. I began to drown in the tremendous sadness of a shattered, lifelong dream.

How did things go so terribly wrong? Dating practically since grade school, we'd been inseparable—our families attended the same church and were best friends. Photo albums filled with hundreds of picture perfect, happy times together hung on our walls. Then why did this initially romantic home became a place of tears, pain and self pity? This was my fairy tale ending? My "perfect" marriage of six months now leaves me feeling like a miserable failure?

I hadn't even eaten breakfast yet, and already had indigestion, disgusted with myself for having allowed my esteem and self worth to dwindle to almost nothing. I had begun to believe his humiliating and degrading comments. He'd all but engraved it in my soul: no one would ever want me because I was too skinny and ugly.

Scarred emotionally and physically from his angry raging verbal and physical attacks, I still prayed that he would soon realize his hurtful behavior and CHANGE. I thought I could be the one to assist him in breaking free from his misguided anger. I naively imagined that I would salvage my marriage by keeping his behavior secret while playing the role of the loving wife.

Something came over me on this near spring morning. As I cut up his french toast I began to detect more than the aroma of the sweet syrup. I could actually smell the sweet fragrance of freedom. I suddenly knew that this was the day I would make my escape from this prison of "love."

This was the day I would finally tell my family what had been going on all this time—why I never visited them or my dying grandmother. This was the day that I was going to walk away with only a few articles of clothing and $4.35 in my pocket. And yet, I would feel like the richest person alive.

As soon as my husband came out of the shower. I presented him with my final gift—his french toast. I strove to be as "normal" as possible, and hid my fear and uneasy anticipation as best I could. If he knew my plan to escape, he would undoubtedly beat me once more, maybe even kill me.

As he left for work, he barked his usual instructions: "Don't watch any television, don't make any phone calls, and don't tell anyone about this or you'll be dead…." When I closed the door behind him, I took a deep, hugely cleansing breath and ran up the stairs to the telephone.

I punched in the number, and when my mom answered I remember crying into the phone "if someone doesn't come and get me, you may never see me again!"

I heard her panicked but determined response, "We'll be right over…" It seemed like an eternity as I grabbed a few items of clothing and waited. My mother and my brother showed up quickly, and I can still feel their secure and comforting hugs. I am ever grateful to them both for their desire to protect me and for rescuing me from my physical and emotional prison.

My arrival at my parents' house was followed by days and days of tears, war stories, and the nurturing love of my family.

That year, as spring flowers came alive, I felt completely dried up. How did my dream of marrying Prince Charming and living happily ever after crash and burn into such a torturous and abusive relationship that—by the time I left—had drained me of almost every facet of my life force?

In the meantime, my husband called frantically, over and over and over again. His parents called as well. When he came to the door, my father answered and, choked up, made the tough emotional decision to send his son-in-law away.

The next year was a blur of restraining orders, lawyer visits, and counseling sessions—all amid a backdrop of letters, presents and flowers that arrived nearly daily. And through it all, lots of introspection.

Now on my own, I acquired a social work position at a facility that housed geriatric and psychiatric patients, as well as juveniles. I looked forward to each day and to helping others feel respected, loved and cared for. I discovered the blessings of simple smiles, warm touches on the hand and loving hugs. What a delight to greet my patients each day.

Finally, two years passed after the "escape" from my marriage, and I'd all but written men off. Out with a co-worker one night, a man approached me to ask if I had any Vicks Vapo Rub. I thought to myself, what kind of an opening line is *that?*

Later on he told me he sensed that I probably needed to laugh more, and that he was trying to lighten up my spirits. I discovered to my surprise that he had quite an interesting sense of humor and a passion for music and poetry. He charmed me with a beautiful sensitivity that kept me talking on the phone many nights into the wee hours of the morning.

He respected the fact that I was reserved. I'll never forget the time that he left a note in my apartment that said: "I don't care if it takes an industrial strength sewing machine to mend your wounds…I'm here for you…" He reinforced the notion that I could be lovable to someone outside of my family. We married nearly three years later, and I'm enormously grateful for this blessing in male form.

On top of being a talented musician and cook (he loves to share his amazing dishes!) he understands my boldness, independence and assertiveness. He's been there for me every step of the way, and his love and attention has proved a soothing balm for my still healing wounds. God bless him and our three beautiful daughters, the flowers of our love.

The Power of Forgiveness

Through it all, I continued my journey toward wholeness. One day while at a health fair, I discovered a book that related the healing story of a woman diagnosed with a basketball size tumor in her uterus.

As I read, I began to experience waves of emotion— rage, sadness, and ultimately understanding and compassion. What I didn't expect is that I would eventually feel forgiveness—for my ex-husband! And when I embarked on a guided visualization process, I found myself asking *him* for forgiveness and blessings.

It was a course called the No Ego Retreat that changed my life most profoundly. Here I discovered that we are all basically born one of nine types. As the group engaged in various exercises and processes to uncover our individual ego fixations, I learned that I was a Number Two, commonly referred to as the "Helper/Giver."

Twos always want to be GOOD. They tend to ignore negative feelings. Twos think that love means always taking care of others—to the point of self-sacrifice. There's usually a lot of martyrdom and low self esteem going on. This described me perfectly.

Twos focus on the opinions of others to affirm and prove their worthiness. Therefore, they spend their lives trying to make people love them, and allow others to have their way easily. I particularly identified with the suppression of personal desires so as not to appear selfish.

Forgetting their own needs, Twos live with a badge of honor that says: "I'm the loving, generous, good and selfless friend who will make you happy and help you solve all of your problems." Eventually Twos can become resentful and blame others for their circumstances. What a huge wake up call for me!

I learned that the blame I had passed onto my ex-husband really was my responsibility too. I learned that everything that happens to us is a mirror reflection of our thoughts about ourselves and about life in general. Even though my ex-husband's abusive behavior could not be condoned, I allowed myself to understand that he was merely an actor in my "play of life" and I opened up to the power of forgiveness and the divine order of life.

I returned home from this retreat filled with enormous compassion for all types of personalities. Realizing that everyone operates out of the pain of their ego fixation was quite an eye-opener!

Since that time I have been humbly honored to become a presenter for the Worldwide Journey Organization, and have been certified as a Visionary Leadership Coach by Conscious Company.

My career involves helping others uncover the sparkling diamonds inside of *their* personal circumstances. I've enthusiastically co-founded several holistic centers in New Jersey that provide a variety of health services and seminars for our clients.

I love God, I love people, and while serving the world, I continue to thank Him for His unending Grace. He has given me the necessary strength and courage to carry me through each day.

I focus on His lessons of love and forgiveness and share these with others in my personal and professional life. It's true that God works in mysterious ways…I now understand that my true purpose in life could only have been revealed to me through my abusive experience years before. The "prison" in which I'd been trapped has now become my beautiful flower-filled garden of passion and purpose. I am truly grateful!

ABOUT THE AUTHOR: Ginny Caroselli has been a social worker for many years as well as holistic health counselor. She is a certified Visionary Leadership Coach for Conscious Company and an authentically dynamic seminar presenter for The Journey. Private and group seminars cover all aspects of Leadership, Conscious Living, and Emotional Clearing. Ginny is Co-Founder of the Mt. Tabor Healing Center in Morris Plains, NJ. She's received the honor of "Woman of the Year" from The National Association of Women Business Owners. Her greatest personal honor is a 27 year marriage to Joe and being the mother of three lovely and amazing daughters.

Ginny Caroselli
www.GinnysJourneys.com
973-703-7318

The Reluctant Psychic
Barbara Davis Elmer

As a young child I rarely slept the whole night through. If it wasn't a dream that awakened me in the middle of the night, I frequently sensed a presence, saw cloudy, shadowy figures, or heard muffled voices talking.

I did not know what they wanted. I only knew that they wanted to communicate with me.

Waking up in the middle of night became routine. While my experiences weren't all bad--I have vivid memories of feeling love and comfort around me, I nevertheless feared these unexpected and often unwelcome "visits."

To me, the connection between spirit-life and this life always seemed worlds apart. Perhaps that explains why I resisted my gifts for so many years. In fact, I actually fled from spiritual connection—I thought that by refusing to see, to *know*, I could also flee from the responsibility of being "my own person."

I did not share this information with many people, and the ones I did share it with laughed at me or thought I was crazy, or worse yet, evil. It didn't take me long to figure out that most people were not like me.

Paralyzed by fear, I closed down a huge part of me, and in so doing, did not realize that I was shutting off the possibilities of who I could *become*. I just wanted to be like everyone else.

At the same time, I questioned everything I experienced. I'd busy myself to keep distracted so that I wouldn't second guess events and situations in my life. By blocking this part of me, I became safe from the power that such ability might wield, and from looking honestly at who and what I was.

Please Don't Let Me be Misunderstood…

Shy and awkward as a child, I always felt misunderstood. I grew to be an unsure and self-conscious adult, which only fueled my passion to be "normal" and accepted. But how could I be? I knew things would happen before they actually did. And I talked to dead people!

I grew up in a large military family, dysfunctional in every sense of the word. My life seemed a perpetual struggle, and survival a way of life. From childhood on I believed that neither joy nor abundance were a part of my destiny. When I married an abusive man, I remained stuck in that place of despair that was so familiar to me. I had no reason to trust in my future, life always failed me.

I tried desperately to find my niche in life. But there seemed to be no shortage of people or situations to remind of my short-comings. Confusion about my place in the world only added to my feelings of defeat and pushed my self-esteem even lower. Often these feelings caused periods of anxiety, panic attacks and depression. And every time I picked myself up, it seemed that something knocked me down again.

The lowest points in my life connected me to suffering and death. My sister Connie, who battled drug addiction most of her life, overdosed on a combination of methadone and several other drugs. Meanwhile, my other sister Pam succumbed to the debilitating effects of multiple sclerosis, complicated by a prior serious car accident.

I stood by them both until their deaths. Pam's life ended at midnight on Christmas Eve. And when my father, who suffered from Parkinson's disease for many years, passed away, my sense of loss and despair became greater still.

This all happened within the span of a few short years. And, as if there wasn't enough death and sorrow in my life, one brother-in-law committed suicide, another passed away in a diabetic coma, and yet a third died from an accidental overdose. Now it seems inevitable that my brother will be next. Homeless, schizophrenic, and a methadone addict, to this day his life hangs in the balance.

While illness, suicide and death factored so heavily into my past, I saw no reason to believe my future would be any different. Defeated, hopeless and confused, there seemed no point to put much faith in future happiness or, in fact, life itself. Why bother, I reasoned.

Our Truest Life is When We are in Dreams Awake...

Although I never thought much about consulting a psychic medium, one day a good friend suggested I might try it. Nah, I thought. What's the point? But something tugged at me until I could resist no more, and I was driven to go.

What happened at this reading was amazing. Seated across from a small-framed angelic-looking woman with long flowing red hair and large brown eyes, she actually seemed to glow. I listened intently, as she began to tell me things no one else could have known.

First she recounted a conversation I'd had with my father before he passed away; she kept repeating a phrase that my father used countless times during his life. And then she reiterated conversations I'd had with Pam and Connie--things I'd shared only with one or the other of them as a little girl. Things I'd *never* told anyone else. I was astounded.

Suddenly, and without warning, she said the strangest thing of all. As she leaned forward and looked directly at me, she said "I'm being told you have this gift too!"

To Thine Own Self be True...

Afterwards, when I finally pulled it together enough to climb out of bed (where I'd spent a good portion of the day stunned and restless as thoughts rolled round and round my head), I finally realized that I could no longer deny who I was or what I knew.

Challenged to view my life and experiences from a different perspective, I was now forced to come face to face with a different reality. It was as if everything in my life led up to this moment. The key to my life had turned, finally revealing all that had previously been hidden...

Suddenly I could no longer deny who I was. My quest had begun in earnest. Drawn to a Reiki class, knowing I was finally destined to become the person I was *always* meant to be, my heart began to open, and I became capable of channeling this new knowledge.

Eventually I began to practice as a psychic medium and spiritual teacher, and to help people through my readings. Finally, I had answers, direction and hope! My very first reading provided me with all the inspiration I needed to know that I was on the right track—that my "gift" could touch another person's life in a truly meaningful way.

A clearly distressed older women asked me to contact her son, who'd died just weeks before. Immediately I "saw" a young boy in a wheel chair (with balloons tied to it!) When I shared this vision, she told me she always tied balloons to his wheelchair, as it made him very happy.

Never able to communicate verbally during his life, he was ecstatic to be able to "talk" to his mother through me. He thanked her for all her love, for the care she'd given him during his lifetime. He thanked her for the balloons and hats that he'd loved receiving, and confided things he'd been unable to say during his life.

Her relief was palpable, and as soon as I finished speaking, I could feel her anxiety melting away. I'd confirmed for her that her son was now at peace and in a safe place.

The Only Journey is the Journey Within…

Little by little, as time went on, I began to view my life not as something to fear, but as a series of lessons. I started to value people and to enjoy the small things in life. Instinctively I knew it was time to embrace the knowledge of a life-time: that my life lessons had prepared me for my calling—as a psychic medium, spiritual teacher, and inspirer of hope!

Now that I've opened my eyes to my spiritual gifts, I've been blessed. As I teach, write, perform readings, and connect people with loved ones who have passed over, I see why I had to go through two divorces, family members' deaths, and other tough situations which at the time seemed both unfair and unbearable.

My past experiences have led me to cultivate an understanding of sensitive circumstances, and the value of people and their pain. It brings me joy to enhance their lives by helping them break through belief systems that hold them back from living a truly full life.

This shifting of awareness allowed me to hone my skills and to dedicate myself to my true calling. Acceptance of the fact that I am psychic medium who helps other people find and connect to their spiritual side has made me happier now than I ever thought possible.

The realization that we are all the same, and all connected on a certain spiritual level, led me to understand that all those years of yearning to be accepted as "normal" were simply a guidepost pointing the way to my own sense of spirituality. As I work toward realizing my full spiritual potential, I know that we are all one, and that it is my right to have abundance, just as it is the right of every human being.

We all carry the seeds of a happy, joyful life. I needed only to overcome my resistance in order to nurture, grow, and embrace the true essence of who and what I am inside.

My guard down, my portals open, I am now the reluctant psychic no more!

ABOUT THE AUTHOR: Barbara's work as a Psychic, Medium, and Reiki Master centers on empowerment and positive forward movement. She conducts classes, workshops, and in-person and telephone readings for those who seek guidance, insight, healing, and spiritual direction. "Each of us has the profound ability to connect and receive answers," Barbara explains. She provides clients' with a deeper understanding of their past, and offers insights that help clarify their future. Barbara works with her guides and angels, and communicates with those who have passed over, to deliver uplifting messages that empower clients with a sense of free will, healing and peace.

Barbara Davis Elmer
www.Barbaraelmer.com
Barbaraelmer111@gmail.com

Endless Possibilities

Roselle Farina-Hecht

I walked down the church aisle carrying a lighted candle in Charlie's memory. When I reached the altar, I handed the candle to the priest and released my husband into God's hands.

This chapter in my life concluded in the very place I had often sat alone and asked for guidance and help. It wasn't until after I reflected upon my experience that I recognized how powerful it was for me. I was free. I let go knowing that Charlie was where he needed to be—with God. Now it was my time to find a way to enjoy the journey that had begun to unfold.

The world as I knew it ended when the man I loved died. It was Easter 2001, a time of new beginnings, a time of death and re-birth. But where could we find the joy of re-birth in my now fatherless daughter's life? Where was there hope, knowing Charlie wouldn't be there to see Nicole reach her life's milestones?

Burying a person I loved taught me much about life. Forced to close a chapter that had been filled with so many dreams that would now never come true, I wept for a life that was no longer mine. At the time, I had no idea why I was going through such a painful life-changing experience. I only knew that, as I mourned, my tears seemed to wash away my dreams; I was powerless to change that.

As the tenth year anniversary of Charlie's death approaches, I decided to reflect on the person I'd become. I know that all the therapy, journaling, conversations, support groups, and praying had prepared me for what lay ahead.

Fabulous Fifty

When I was in my early forties, I determined I'd be enjoying life again by the age of fifty. My goal was to be happy with myself at that age, and I made the decision to try to find out how to fix me; I knew I was broken.

The thought of fixing all that was wrong with me by the age of fifty was overwhelming! Most of all I decided I wanted to be happy at fifty. The process wasn't easy—my self exploration was painful, yet rewarding.

At first it was quite a challenge to recognize and embrace the tools and gifts within. Slowly, I learned to open myself up to the gifts of each day; I learned to grow as a person. I took a chance and allowed myself to find out what I really wanted in my life. I began to accept that I am responsible for my own destiny.

Charlie had died, and as the summer approached Nicole wanted to go to sleep away camp. I discovered a wellness center program that I decided to attend and, after I dropped my daughter at camp, I suddenly pulled the car over to the side of the road. Uncontrollable tears poured out of me, as the recognition that I no longer had a spouse ripped through me once again. Reality hit: I was alone…

I sought solace and comfort in my dear friend Diana Black. She'd visited me the morning after Charlie died to offer comfort, assistance and food. Diana and I had met at a support group for adoptive parents when our daughters were toddlers, and later the girls attended the same Catholic elementary school.

My friendship with Diana grew over the years, and we often confided our life experiences to one another. We shared the belief that we were both "old souls." Now she again provided me with support and love. She was willing to drive miles to rescue me if necessary. Diana encouraged me to continue with my plans no matter how scared I felt. We both knew the program would help my healing process.

As that summer reached its end, I heard Melissa Etheridge's song "I Want To Be In Love." As I listened, the words began to resonate within me. I wanted to feel love again. I needed to stop crying and to live again. My daughter's sophomore year in high school began to fill with school activities—homework, soccer, school dances. She was learning how to enjoy life without a father.

What was I going to do with *my* life?

Fred called and asked me to meet him for a cup of coffee at Starbucks. We'd known each other for almost two decades. He was safe. Since I had known him for years, I knew about his work. He believed in giving back to society. He was interesting. I decided to open up my heart and met him for coffee…

When Fred made me laugh, I felt the connection! I wanted to know more about him. Fred, too, had struggled through a lot of issues. Death had robbed him of loved ones as well, and turned his life upside down. Forced to look deeply into his soul to figure out what he wanted from life, Fred definitely was someone to whom I could relate to on my journey. I decided he was the person I needed to be with as I continued on my path of self exploration.

I celebrated my fiftieth birthday with family and friends. I gave Nicole the gift of a mom filled with joy. I invited everyone to join me at a Staten Island Yankees' baseball game. The stadium features an amazing view of New York City. As we watched the game, we were also treated to a fabulous view of the ships moving calmly along on the water.

That day I received a very special gift from Fred, who continued to make me laugh and smile at the world. To make my birthday even more special, Fred took me to a castle. As my fiftieth birthday drew to a close, I fell asleep—a princess in a castle! A magical experience, even for one who considers herself a down to earth successful business woman…

When the man who'd made me feel like a princess on my fiftieth birthday told me he wanted to spend the rest of his life with me, I knew that I was about to embark on an amazing adventure. Surrounded by family and friends, Fred and I became husband and wife. As we both broke glasses under the chupah, it marked the beginning of a new life for two individuals who would never have dreamed this special day could ever have been possible.

Turning the Corner

Empowered now with the knowledge that I could make my own choices, I learned that I was responsible for myself only, and not everyone else in my life. A support group that I attended during my forties discussed how important it was to take care of "self." At the time, I'd heard the message but didn't really understand what it meant.

The bond between Nicole and me has grown stronger as she matures into a successful woman. When I took my daughter and her friends to the theater when she was young, I told them, "you can be anything you want to be." It was so easy to say those words to them, but I never stopped to apply them to myself!

As a mother, my role was to teach and guide Nicole, not to control her. I wanted to empower her with the knowledge that, for a young woman, the world was filled with limitless possibilities. Just as I'd learned so much about myself, I hoped my daughter was learning too.

I laugh a lot now. I enjoy reading books. The media and books expose me to a universe I'm hungry to explore. There is a most amazing world out there, and I am enjoying it more as I begin to live my dreams.

When I went to Egypt I took a boat ride down the Nile, and remembered all the biblical stories on which I'd been raised. When I visited the ruins of Pompeii, I thought: "I am walking the streets I've seen in books and on television." Left speechless as I roamed through the rooms where Anne Frank lived, I couldn't believe I was in the actual space that she'd shared with me in her diary. The words on a page now penetrated through me as I wandered from room to room. Travel became interwoven into the fabric of my life.

When I ask myself what I want to feel "when I close my eyes for the last time" the answer is joy and happiness. I want to see more of the world, be with the people I love, and to read, explore, and expand! My education is an integral part of who I am today.

At the beginning of this year, I said goodbye to my dear and special friend Diana. I recalled the day when, home alone battling cancer, Diana fell. As she lay on the floor, unable to get up, she heard my voice on her answering machine. I had no idea she needed help; I just knew I had to call her that day. She told me later how much comfort she'd felt just in hearing my voice.

Her daughter Jennifer found her a little later and took her to the hospital. In church, friends and family prayed together as her draped casket held her in our midst. I realized again that my life will end one day too.

It wasn't easy when I started the process. The path wasn't clearly marked. Yet as I explored what I really wanted for myself, I became more open to the various possibilities I encountered on my journey.

Today a pile of books sit on my night stand. My iPad opens up an endless world of downloads for me! How will I ever find all the time necessary to continue to learn about myself?

While life doesn't always seem to work out the way we plan, I now know one thing for sure: If we can do what it takes to let go, life will unfold with its own wonderful, unpredictable force, and present to us the most miraculous events and experiences in the most unimaginable ways...

ABOUT THE AUTHOR: Roselle was raised in a middle class Italian family in Brooklyn New York. Working full time during some semesters and attending school in the evenings, she accomplished her BA in 4 years. Her extensive business background enabled her to see the endless possibilities of owning her own business. In 1989 she co-founded Staten Island Parent. Today her company produces a monthly parenting magazine, an annual resource guide and a growing website. Her amazing daughter, Nicole, has been the motivation to learn how to combine family and work. Fred, her husband, inspires her to follow her dreams.

Roselle Farina-Hecht
Staten Island Parent
www.siparent.com
Roselle@siparent.com
718-761-4800 x 140

Embrace the Light Within

Caren M. Kolerski

"Come on grandma, you can do it!" I nearly stopped dead in my tracks. I thought I'd heard "come on Caren, you can do it! I'm proud of you and I'm supporting you!"

And the voice I thought I'd heard was that of my mother speaking words I'd longed to hear for more than thirty years!

In reality, it was my five year old granddaughter calling to me from the top of the slide at the local playground. My spirit responded to her courage and fearlessness as I accepted her invitation, climbed the steps of the ladder and enjoyed the ride back down!

With the wisdom so often inherent in innocence, she knew just what I needed.

My own mother's sudden and early death at the age of forty had cemented my fears and insecurities at a young age. Her critical and demanding voice still rang in my mind, and far outweighed the much fainter memory of gentle and supportive love.

Times of hugs and stories told to me on her lap were vastly overshadowed by memories of imposed limitations and her demand that tasks and chores be completed to perfection. My self-esteem and confidence level grew about as high as a step-stool.

Pieces of the puzzle began to come to light during the Heal Your Life® certification training I completed over a decade ago. Based on the philosophy of Louise L Hay, renowned author and spiritual teacher, that as you change your thoughts you can heal your life, I realized I needed to heal myself from the inside out.

I sobbed during a song played for a mirror exercise as I began to look deeply into my soul. I knew then it was time to take the journey.

I grieved and released over two decades of bottled up tears, remnants of my often turbulent relationship with my mother, as well as those of the vast unknown territory of adult womanhood I traveled alone.

No surprise as the "thanks, but no thanks!" letters arrived following my job interviews. Glowing references written on paper could not override the story my body language revealed.

My head understood the concepts at motivational seminars for business building, but still I wasn't able to reach my dream of entrepreneurship: to earn a great income and live a full, happy and successful life…

What was holding me back? I realized it was my own sense of self-esteem as I recounted in my mind the thoughts I so often repeated to myself: "I don't deserve abundance" and "it has to be hard," for starters. And let's not forget "people will leave me if I am successful," "who will listen to *me*? And "it's already been said!"

I knew I wanted to live larger but my fear paralyzed me. I was breathing and functioning, but not fully alive. I felt trapped, like the Chilean miners must have felt, buried in the depths of darkness a mile or so below the surface of the earth.

My heart beat but I had no real passion for anything…Often frustrated, the truth finally became clear: my thoughts needed some serious upgrading! I began working with my mind to turn off that nagging, critical voice that still vibrated within me and sometimes found its way out of my mouth. I learned to affirm myself with different, more positive language.

"I love and approve of myself as I am" became my mantra, sometimes hundreds of times a day! My recovery included listening daily to affirmative CDs while striving forward on the treadmill. I began to understand that my mother had done the best she could as she made her way through life, having absorbed similar vibrations from her own mother. And so I learned to forgive.

"It is Our Light, Not Our Darkness That Most Frightens Us." ~ Marianne Williamson

I thought I'd learned my healing lessons in regard to my mother until those haunting vibrations once again found their way into my brain while on a mini retreat.

I happened to gaze at a picture of myself holding a white dove about to be released in honor of my fifty years on this planet, and recalled my sense of awe and wonder as I looked into its eyes, listened to its cooing, and felt it's every vibration.

It was as if I truly connected with this amazing creature, just like I had connected with my granddaughter when we met for the first time as she lay in my arms, less than one hour old.

I wondered if my mother ever felt that same sense of awe and wonder for *me* and, if she did, why I never really felt or heard it? While I lay in her womb, did she caress me and let me know how much she'd grown to love me? Would she miss me once I was no longer her twenty-four hour companion? Tears flooded my cheeks; I knew beyond a shadow of a doubt where my issue lay. *This* was where the dark cloud seemed to be hovering; I felt stuck.

The work I had done was not wasted, however; it had prepared me to go deeper. I had never felt that precious mother-daughter connection. How I longed for her to take my face in her hands when it was filled with acne, or when I felt so ugly—like a creature from another planet— wearing a back brace to junior high school.

It was her attention I craved when I was "caught" in the cookie jar, or refrigerator, looking for something to fill me up—I only wanted her to tell me how beautiful I was...no matter what! The vibration of fear I'd carried for five decades rose to the surface. I felt my body shudder as if my face was still going to be slapped.

More tears of release flowed. I held my face in my hands and hugged myself tenderly to sooth the lost, frightened little girl inside and assure her I would always love her and care for her deeply—no matter what. I would *always* be there for her!

Finally, after so many years, I had found the missing link to my success—loving MYSELF! My emotional self welcomed this knowledge like a drought welcomes the rain. I felt calm like the ocean's depth, like nothing I'd ever known before…

This time I was not afraid of the tears; I simply allowed them to fall knowing that I had been through it before and was safe. It was for my highest good. Now I was able to understand more fully who I am—I am peace, joy, laughter and love!

It was there all the time, just waiting for me to let go of the "stuff" that was blocking my vision. What I sought was actually inside seeking ME! I felt GOOD about me; I esteemed and valued myself for who I am on the inside!

This is why I was created—to fully love myself, and to help others see their own magnificence! My spirit knew I was ready to begin my healing process so that I could evolve into the inspired teacher I am today, ready to embrace all who are drawn to my light!

In the days that followed, as my granddaughter and I shared a bathroom sink and mirror while we brushed our teeth, I could see the beauty and innocence in her face. After the last swish, I instinctively took her face in my hands and, with great love, told her how beautiful she is! It was a most powerful moment of healing; I had found my inner parent.

From this space of love for myself I now can more fully love others, including my husband, despite his physical and emotional challenges. I realize now that when my critical voice rises up within me and comes out of my mouth, I must breathe, return to love, and nurture myself.

I know now that it's my responsibility. When I become reactive to anyone or anything, I know I am looking in a mirror of what needs to be healed next within me and get to work! I have always wanted to be a teacher and now, through healing myself, I am able to help others from a heart full of love.

There is a great light and an unlimited love within me ready to express as *me* while I live. My passion found me, and if any doubt still remains, I bend down and look in the mirror, as the Christmas tree's blue and green lights reflect in the pupils and irises of my eyes—countless little sparks of light—reminders that I am filled with the Light of the Universe, and echo the familiar phrase: "Remember who you are!"

"And as we let our own light shine, we unconsciously give other people permission to do the same." Marianne Williamson

"What lies behind us and what lies in front of us are of small matter to what lies within us!" Ralph Waldo Emerson

ABOUT THE AUTHOR: Caren M Kolerski, BSW, Buffalo-Niagara native, author, speaker and owner of Heart Wings Healing, is an inspired leader of personal and global transformation. She passionately guides clients —via in-person or telephone coaching sessions, workshops, and Women's retreats — toward expansion of consciousness, growth and success! Experienced as a Life Coach, Licensed Heal Your Life® Workshop Leader, Certified Stress Management Consultant and Laughter Leader, Caren successfully practices what she teaches. Empowering clients to discover their Inner Wisdom and return to their natural state of happiness, health, love, peace, joy and prosperity is Caren's mission. This IS the time!

Caren M. Kolerski
www.Pathway2Presence.com
coachcaren@gmail.com
716-983-7714

Do You Hear What I Hear?

Caly Lehrer

I can still hear my father's loud, guttural laugh reverberating throughout the room after I told him my exciting news. A laugh so loud it felt like the cold cement floor that lay beneath me shook in unison with his thunderous laugh.

As he pulled back his gold rimmed glasses to wipe a tear from his eye, the man who I trusted and adored more than anyone on earth looked at me and exclaimed, "YOU CANNOT TALK WITH THE ANIMALS!"

Although I was always the perfect child who never spoke back, this time I defiantly snapped, "YES I CAN!"

As my father walked away to go back to his TV, I sat down on the cold basement floor in front of my childhood dog, Ginger. Although not sure why, I felt the need to console her; I wished she hadn't heard those words.

Ginger's brown cock-a-poo eyes, softly met mine; flecks of love and compassion shone brightly, yet with a twinge of sorrow mixed in. She sensed what was about to happen. In a way, we were saying good-bye to a precious gift we had shared.

Instinctively, I knew I couldn't withstand the ridicule. If my own father could laugh at me with such robust and piercing ridicule, surely the scorn of others would leave far worse scars. There in the darkness of a damp, cold basement, I clung to Ginger's body, now a tissue absorbing my tears. I whispered "I love you," as a part of me shut down and died. Yet deep down inside, the truth remained...I *can* talk with the animals.

As I grew from a child into a woman, I didn't give talking with the animals much thought. Like so many other painful memories from my childhood, I swept that heart-wrenching memory with Ginger under the rug. Yet throughout my life, one thing remained constant…I always felt a strong bond and love for dogs.

I understood dogs, and they seemed to understand me. For me, there was no greater gift than spending time in the presence of a dog. No human ever seemed able to give me what dogs so easily shared…the immeasurable gift of their unconditional love.

I never felt like I fit in, so there was no greater feeling than knowing I could be loved so unconditionally. Whenever I cried, my dogs were right there to kiss away my tears. If I was in the midst of jubilant celebration, my dogs were there, jumping on my shoulders as their tails danced in the air, sharing in my happiness. When it came to my dogs, I was always loved and accepted "as is."

In my mid-thirties my life took an unexpected turn. Although afflicted with fibromyalgia for many years, I suddenly became drastically ill. Pain shot through my right side with every breath I took, and I looked white as a ghost.

After a battery of tests, the doctors discovered that I was suffering from previously undetected herniated thoracic discs, and now some of my organs were in danger of shutting down. Rushed into emergency surgery, my doctors were forced to collapse a lung, fracture my right rib cage and pull it apart to get to the herniated discs.

I was left with a long road of healing. Yet right there by my side was my faithful dog, Tippy, a beautiful cocker spaniel.

Due to the size and location of the surgical incision, sleeping proved to be quite a challenge. Unable to lay on my front, back or right side, mountains of pillows were propped all around me in an effort to keep me immobilized during the night.

One night—in the midst of a fitful sleep—I rolled onto my right side, and horrific pain woke me instantly. Still very weak and in great pain, I couldn't undo my careless move. In the dark of night, I yelled out for my mom, who was staying over to care for me.

Yet with my mom sound asleep in the guest bedroom, my cries for help went unheard. Lying on the floor beside me, snug in her bed, Tippy realized my plight. She jumped out of bed, pushed her way through the bedroom door, and determinedly made her way to my mom's room.

Tippy scratched at the door with her fluffy paw, and I was soon comforted by the sound of my mother's voice, "What's the matter Tippy? Is everything alright?" With my mom now awake, she heard my cries as Tippy led her to my side. After my mom helped me roll over onto my left side, we both praised Tippy for what she'd just done.

Several months later, my doctor thought I should consider going on more medication. Having been on heavy doses of medication for far too long, I was reluctant to go on even more. I looked at my doctor and from somewhere deep down inside, I confidently said, "I think I'll try a holistic approach."

As the words came out, I wondered where they came from. I wasn't even sure what holistic meant! Then the very next day, as God would have it, a brochure arrived in the mail; Reiki classes were being offered in a neighboring town. Although I had heard of Reiki, I really didn't know much about it; yet since the brochure said you could give Reiki to yourself, I figured I'd give it a try.

I immersed myself in Reiki and my healing began to improve. Tippy stood by me every step of the way, as I slowly climbed the upward hill towards healing. Inseparable, Tippy and I did everything together. I never felt a greater love than I did with my beloved Tippy.

As my body continued to heal, people began to tell me how good I was at sharing Reiki. Knowing what a difference it made in my life, I opened up to the idea of sharing Reiki with others. As my confidence grew, I decided to start my own Reiki business.

As always, Tippy was right by my side when I worked each day. With her long, floppy ears, she'd eagerly wiggle her stub-tailed butt, exuberantly greet each client and put them at ease. Tippy had helped me with my healing journey, and now she was helping so many others.

Over time, Tippy's health began to fail. Throughout the years, I always told people proudly how Tippy had the hugest heart. And although innocently spoken, I quickly learned the power of our words. Tippy was eventually diagnosed with congestive heart disease. My little girl had an enlarged heart; her unconditionally loving heart had grown too big! It was now my turn to care for Tippy the way she had selflessly cared for me throughout some of my hardest years.

Despite her challenges, Tippy remained my teacher. Her health issues guided me to start sharing Reiki with her. And through that connection, I grew to realize my true passion was working with animals. With Tippy as my "guinea pig," I practiced sharing Reiki with her, and together we learned a lot. And although it seemed impossible, our bond strengthened even more.

Christmas came and passed, and it was time for me to take down our tree. It was a weekday and I happened to be home alone. Late in the day, on a cold winter's afternoon, I slowly began to un-trim the tree. With empty boxes scattered around me, I first took down the silver star that crowned the tree. I neatly tucked away the garland, made from beads of blue. Then one by one, down came each precious ornament.

Every year I traditionally bought Tippy a new Hallmark® ornament for the tree; each one had a slot for a picture. Before packing the ornaments away for the year, I reminisced about the happy memory each one held. There were so many happy memories!

As I continued to work, late afternoon turned into evening darkness, and all the while Tippy lay curled up on the couch, fast asleep. With all the ornaments now packed away, I sat before a stark green tree. I remember vividly how the barren tree stood in front of our big picture window, with the darkness of a cold winter night looming in the background.

As the cold air penetrated the windows I thought of pulling the blinds before I packed the tree. Suddenly Tippy awoke, jumped from the couch, and ran over to sit beside me. Resting against my right ribcage where my surgery had been, she sat in silence, her gaze intently fixed on the tree.

Minutes passed, yet she remained totally still, front and center, just staring at the tree. Somewhat baffled, I looked over and asked, "What…what is it girl?" Then as clear as could be I heard her whisper these words, "I want to look at the tree one more time before you put it away…it's the last time I'm going to see it."

With warm tears streaming down my face, I sat alone with my dog in the darkness, just like I had as a little girl, only this time on a cold wooden floor. And although the words were hard to hear, I knew I couldn't shut them down. Side-by-side, we sat in silence and stared out at the tree. A tree without decorations, a tree without lights, became the most beautiful Christmas tree I'd ever seen. Love had come full circle.

Two and a half months later, my beloved girl Tippy left this earth. The last thing she saw as she passed from this world into the next, were my eyes bravely staring into her fearful brown ones. Assuring her we'd be together forever, I whispered, "I love you."

In the midst of her pain, Tippy remained a teacher and healer. She gently tore the veil from the truth that had been buried deep down inside since so long ago…I *can* talk with the animal.

ABOUT THE AUTHOR: As Your Spiritual Guardian For Animal Wellness, Caly Lehrer's passion is working with Animals and the Humans who care for them. Caly is a Reiki Master/Teacher, Accredited Journey™ Practitioner, Visionary Leadership Coach, Empathic Intuitive and Animal Communicator. Using these gifts and more, Caly strives to restore balance and well-being with Abuse/Neglect, Pet Loss/Bereavement, Compassion Fatigue, and Physical, Emotional or Behavioral challenges. Because animals take on so many of our emotions, Caly's commitment is to work with you to be the best you can be for your personal well-being, as well as that of our Animal Friends.

Caly Lehrer
Peace-By-Peace, LLC
www.PeaceByPeace.net
Caly@PeaceByPeace.net
303-862-5424

Magical Mystical Tour
Kumari Mullin

"Try to not be disappointed in anything. Know that life is showing up perfectly in every moment. Today's disappointment could be tomorrow's springboard to all that you've ever wanted. In fact, it probably is." ~Neale Donald Walsh

Every morning Nellie Bly sat cross-legged on the bed, her eyes closed, and exuded a calm that eluded the rest of us. Curious, one day I asked her what she was doing. "Meditating" she replied simply.

Though I'd heard the word before, I didn't know anyone who meditated. So I asked her what meditation did for her, and she answered with this story:

"On my way to work one morning, something made me suddenly pull a U-turn across the highway and race back home. When I got there, all the doors and windows were bolted, so I had to break in. I found my roommate lying on the floor, unconscious, with a bottle of pills beside her, and called the ambulance. They pumped her stomach and told me I'd saved her life."

I recall thinking "that's what I want"—I didn't even know what to call it then—that ability to just *know* on a very deep level and to act in a way that can literally save lives. But I had no clue where to go to learn to meditate, and soon dropped the idea.

I'd met Nelly Bly shortly after graduating from college in 1982, when I volunteered to work for the historic last ditch effort to pass the Equal Rights Amendment (ERA). I was one of four lucky women chosen to travel the state of Oklahoma and do advance work for actor Alan Alda, a wonderful advocate for women's equality.

After the E.R.A failed to pass, I still felt committed to advocate for change but this time hoped for a bit more clout. I decided to go to Washington, D.C., and become a lawyer. Dedicated to speaking up for those who could not, I joined Legal Aid where I represented developmentally disabled individuals in state institutions. Though intensely challenging, I found the civil rights work deeply rewarding.

Just as my legal career began to take off, my father became ill. At first he thought it was pneumonia, but the x-rays showed he had lung cancer. Only sixty, he'd been happily planning to travel and "see America." Instead, in a few short months he ended up in intensive care fighting for his life.

One night at four o'clock in the morning I bolted upright from my bed and undeniably heard the words "he is not coming home from the hospital." Though I wanted to remain positive, every cell of my being knew it was true.

My father, a surgeon, had everyone convinced he was going to leave the hospital soon and that we should wait until he was home to visit. I prevailed upon my siblings to ignore his urgings to wait, and instead to fly in immediately. Thankfully, we all managed to be there with him during his last weeks.

I sat at his bedside in the ICU and remember feeling incredibly useless until the nurse brought out some lemon glycerin lollipops. Finally, I could swab my father's parched cracked lips, and offer him a moment of reprieve from the incredible challenge presented by each raggedy breath. But I still could not shake the vague desire to do so much MORE for him.

On July 18, 1988, I kissed my father goodbye and he strained to whisper "I love you." I walked down the hall and heard the code. He was conscious right up until the moment he left his body.

Piercing The Veil

The loss of my father felt like a buffer zone of protection from the harshness of the world was gone. Shortly after returning to work, a colleague of mine at Legal Aid introduced me to her meditation master from India, and I recalled Nellie Bly and my intention years earlier to learn meditation.

Many spiritual seekers expend a lot of effort to find their teacher, but there is a saying that "when the student is ready, the master appears." That certainly was the case for me.

One door closes, another opens. Looking back, I don't think I would've been open to this strange new universe filled with gurus, practices of chanting in ancient Sanskrit languages, meditating for hours while sitting cross-legged, the study of obscure ancient spiritual texts, the dizzying pranayama practices, and yoga at three a.m.! But the loss of my father catapulted me into the need to understand death and dying, and a deep desire to alleviate suffering.

My logical lawyer mind began to open to experiences of incredible ecstasy (non-pharmaceutical!), amazing insight, profound other-worldly wisdom, and unexplained phenomenon that transcended ordinary senses.

I felt so high in the presence of the guru, it startled me. All I wanted was to be near her incandescence. From the first time I watched her on a video, I felt something strange inside…like the butterflies of a schoolgirl with a crush, only deeper. Spellbound every time she looked into the camera, I felt like she could see right into my soul.

She spoke of things of which I'd never heard…like awakening the kundalini energy dormant at the base of the spine. It happened almost instantly—I experienced the classic eastern spiritual awakening, complete with vivid light shows, amazing visions, spontaneous yoga postures, and tremendous physical sensations, including a profound sense of connection and oneness.

I also started to become aware of the healing capacity in my hands. I knew if I placed them on someone their headache would disappear. I found this a bit disturbing, however. But then I discovered an ancient energy healing art called Reiki, and signed up. When I'd completed my first seminar, I instantly knew I was home.

Less than a year later, I felt guided to leave the law. With no job and no idea what I was going to do, everyone thought I had lost my marbles. My poor family worried I'd joined a Jonestown cult and freaked out!

My mother called her friend's brother who was a Jesuit priest and described to him what I'd been doing. Amazingly, the priest responded: "Did you ever consider that your daughter might be a holy woman?" After that, she calmed down a wee bit.

A close friend had another concern: "You're not really grieving your father's death," she warned me. I thought—why grieve—he is sitting right next to me! I'd opened up to the world of spirit, and experienced my father with me more often than not.

One day, I felt his strong presence in the car with me as I drove alone with the radio on. We both loved music, and some of my favorite memories were of singing duets with him as a small child. I asked him to give me a sign that it really was him sitting next to me in the passenger seat.

An incredible thing happened. My right hand was on the gear shift and I felt my little pinky finger curl up and lift away from my hand. I had not moved it myself! I began to sob; my father and I had this tradition in church…we would lock our pinkies together in a mini-hug. It was one of the sweetest moments we shared, and my whole family adopted this tender mini-embrace.

This strong connection continued for more than a year. I found that when I called out to my father, I felt his presence every time.

Over the following twenty-two years, I studied and lived with meditation masters, spiritual teachers, and healers in an intense quest to understand illness and death and to discover new ways to ease suffering and *"be peace."*

Some might ask, but at what cost? In order to follow my heart, I left a fulfilling job and respectable career, moved over ten times in one year, and found myself homeless and penniless more than once. I lost friends, and the respect and support of my family at times. And more than one marriage ended as I continued on my quest.

The Journey Comes Full Circle

Today I have no regrets. My journey of the heart endowed me with incredible insight and certitude, and gifted me with amazing teachers, friends, students, and a wonderful partner. My family and friends now accept me and my path, and some have even become my students!

My father's death transformed my life. It highlighted for me the thin veil of separation between the corporeal and spiritual worlds, and enabled me to help pierce that veil for many others. My father's passing opened a portal for me, one that continues to pour blessings on so many lives.

Funny how things come full circle. I now *teach* meditation, intuitive development and healing. I help people find peace in meditation when nothing else they've tried works; I share how to develop intuition and communicate with animals and all of nature; I allow animals to feel they are truly seen and heard on the deepest of levels; I've facilitated healing for thousands of people and animals physically, mentally and emotionally; I empower people to shine their light and be the healers, teachers and leaders they are meant to be; I help people identify their soul purpose, and in so doing I fulfill mine.

What is more, I merged my extreme passion for animals into my intuitive healing practice and I can count among my friends and teachers cougars, dolphins, whales, elephants, gorillas, and king vultures. I now speak comfortably and easily with the very same alligators and wild boars that once frightened me.

For me, this life is nothing short of a "magical mystical tour." It's as if I look through the lens of the heart's window to the universe, where miracles are the norm. When I attempt to discern which ideas are inspired, and which come from the overactive ego mind, I trace my thoughts back to their source, and *feel* from where they originate. The whispers emanating from the cave of the heart are the ones I trust. As one of my revered teachers, Swami Nityananda, profoundly summed it up: *"The heart is the hub of all sacred places; Go there and roam."*

ABOUT THE AUTHOR: Rev. Kumari Mullin, JD is the Founder and CEO of Kumari Healing Inc. As a result of her 22-year personal journey of metaphysical mastery, which included studying and living with internationally acclaimed meditation masters, energy healers and spiritual teachers – including animal communication pioneer Penelope Smith -

she is now an internationally recognized and highly desired expert and teacher specializing in energetic solutions. One internationally recognized spiritual teacher proclaimed: "Kumari's purpose is to Teach the Teachers' Mastery!" As an Author, Professional Speaker, Reiki Master/Teacher, Attorney, Counselor, Animal Intuitive, Retreat Facilitator, Healer and Coach, Kumari has assisted thousands of people and animals worldwide achieve extraordinarily profound transformations.

Kumari Mullin
Kumari Inc.
www.kumarihealing.com
kumari@kumarihealing.com
772-589-9803

The Sound of Crystal Singing

Nanette Nuvolone

The hardest thing I've ever done was to end a relationship with a man I didn't love. I'd felt obligated to stand by his side because there just was never a good time to go. The time was wrong when he became sick with a mysterious illness, wrong when a motorcycle accident badly injured him. I didn't have the courage to leave when his mother died, and felt obligated to support him when he became unemployed.

Now I was finally worthy. I wasn't sure where the courage to speak my truth came from, but I knew it was the first step towards loving me. My heart was ready to unburden my pain. It was time to heal.

The angelic tones of the crystal singing bowls catapulted me into a journey of self discovery one evening as the words "You must love yourself" startled me into focusing on my mission. I was at a place where I'd meet periodically with a community of like-minded individuals, all seeking to "raise our vibration."

So strongly did the message come through that I must finally disabuse myself of the notion that "I don't know how to love," that the tears welled up in my eyes and burned the sides of my checks as they fell hot and fast.

"I don't know how to love." I consistently repeated this affirmation whenever problems in my relationship arose. Why else could I be so unhappy? I didn't have the ability to voice the unhappiness of my unmet needs. Nor did I have the courage to walk away.

Affirmations go beyond the present moment into the creation of the future by the words we use in the now. Ignorant of that fact, I soon learned that affirmations, when combined with the crystal singing bowls, create the ability to bring about a positive shift in our consciousness.

So how do I begin to love myself? It starts with putting me first. The relationship that felt so comfortably wrong needed to end. But how? He needed me more than I deserved to be happy, or so I thought.

Before every crystal singing bowl session I would pick an oracle card. This was a strange concept to a woman with no sense of spirituality who had drifted through life believing that she was not only unable to love, but unable to connect with the divine.

"Take charge" the message read. I needed to give myself permission to do what I felt was right and be clear about what conditions I found acceptable. It was time for me to make a decision instead of waiting passively. So I did. I decided to affirm "I am worthy of the very best in life and I now lovingly allow myself to accept it."

Around this time I was introduced to Louise Hay and her philosophy about life. I started to learn that every person with whom we enter into a relationship mirrors ourselves. We attract certain people into our lives because there are aspects about ourselves that we need to heal. Interesting for me since I always told my boyfriend that the things I loved about him were the things I hated about him. Now I understood why; I had a lot of healing to do.

A Way of Life

So my relationship finally ended and I was free to live. Where did I want to live? What did I want to do with my life? How do I continue to learn to love myself? The answers came after many sessions of raising my vibration with the crystal bowls. Loving *me* meant living somewhere that made me feel good. Where was that place and how would I get there? I figured an affirmation was a great way to start.

"I am open and receptive to a wonderful new position; I live in sunny Florida, and earn a good living." Tired of enduring the cold winter months in New Jersey, I'd wanted to move to Florida for quite some time. I began to search for a job in Florida and even applied for positions well below my level of experience at several companies.

Finally, I threw my hands up in the air and decided that if it was meant to be, it would happen. And so it did. The affirmation worked! My company announced the dissolution of my job in New Jersey and offered me a relocation package for a position in Orlando.

Wow, this couldn't be so easy, could it? In what other areas of my life did I have the power to change, I wondered. Apparently, loving me not only meant having the courage to leave a relationship at the right time, but also to believe that good things could happen for me. Could I be that powerful?

Affirmation became a way of life. I'd spring out of bed in the morning and spontaneously chatter about anything for which I considered myself grateful. Next I would pick an affirmation for the day and write it out ten times. I'd repeat this affirmation throughout the day. I'd reinforce my affirmations through my sessions with the crystal singing bowls.

My connection with the divine began to flourish. I had always felt strongly intuitive, but only when I embarked on doing something that could potentially cause me pain. However, I was now connected on a totally different level.

Suddenly, feathers began to spontaneously appear. Whether they appeared in my mind's eye during meditation, or floated down from the ceiling of the room I entered, it felt amazing to have a divine support system. I began to receive messages about my future. "Your life purpose involves teaching others about healing and spirituality." Really? *Me?*

I anxiously checked the website for the next session dates when I found out I could become certified to teach the Louise Hay philosophy that had changed my life. The only problem was the only session that worked coincided with my cousin's wedding. Do I go to the wedding or attend the training that I desperately wanted? I decided to attend the wedding and forget about the training.

About a month later I received an email notifying me that a new session had been added! The week long training would end right before my sales meeting started in California! Perfect, I thought…not only would I get to attend the training; I wouldn't have to pay for airfare because my company was already flying me to California for our national sales meeting. Ecstatic, I never felt so excited. I'd been searching for meaning for so long, and now I finally knew I was on the right path.

"Doors closing, doors opening, I am safe, it's only change," went the words of the song we listened to during our very first "You can heal your life" teacher training session. With eyes closed, we all sang along. Emotion overwhelmed me and paralyzed my voice. At that moment I embraced the many changes in my life over the past six months. My heart finally open, I was ready to receive.

Surrounded by a cocoon of love the entire week, I began to shed the layers that had inhibited my growth. On the very last day, our workshop leaders arranged for us to visit their ranch for a journey through their labyrinth to close the session. I stated my intention upon entering: guidance. I began to feel fearful as I processed all I'd learned throughout the week.

I slowly followed the path to the center and hoped for a message. I watched the members of my group and felt the love they each radiated as they each exited the labyrinth. I figured the message would come when the time was right, and began to make my way back towards the ranch. As I stumbled to find the correct trail, I heard the familiar sound of my higher self: "You will be led on the right path." I've taken comfort from that moment on that I am guided always in whatever I do.

ABOUT THE AUTHOR: A licensed "Heal Your Life" workshop leader, Nanette holds a Bachelors of Arts in Humanities with a concentration in psychology. Her mission to raise her own consciousness led Nanette to the philosophies of Louise Hay. It was her discovery of Hay's transformational book "You Can Heal Your Life," that inspired her to discard old belief systems, love herself unconditionally, and heal aspects of her life that no longer served a positive purpose. Nanette feels "truly blessed" to be able to inspire and empower others along their spiritual journey to create the lives they truly desire through her workshops.

Nanette Nuvolone
www.nanettenuvolone.com
n_nuvo@hotmail.com
732-677-0593

DOGMA* TO GODMA

Or, A Miracle is Only a Perspective Away
Heather Saline

*Dogma: A doctrine or code of beliefs accepted as authoritative; not to be disputed, doubted or diverged from…

The fact that Schuyler came with special needs did not deter my husband and me from the mission to adopt him and become a family. After all, I had a history of dogged determination and success. His needs would be met. We would be FINE.

But never did I imagine the word "fine" would become synonymous with Chronic, Acute, Impossible and Insanity!

Schuyler was a joyful, bright-eyed and contentedly happy five month old baby boy when we became his parents. Blessed to be able to stay home with him, I never tired of watching his discoveries. We would fly to the moon and back every day! The thrill of motherhood was just as I'd dreamed it would be!

By the time he was one and a half years old, it became clear that Schuyler would not escape the effects of his birth mother's "issues," including suspected mental health illness, recreational *and* therapeutic drug use, and a seizure disorder.

Eventually, we'd be told that Schuyler's special needs did not fall into a category that included proven, effective therapies or medical treatments. By the time he was six, his behaviors—produced by an unstable chemistry—grew to such a challenging level that less than a handful of people were qualified to supervise him.

Days became filled—I mean FILLED—with ear piercing squeals, nerve-wracking claps and bangs, and non-stop moving, running and grabbing. If it was in his hands, it was destroyed within minutes.

I remember one day crying in gratitude; Schuyler watched an entire children's video…it was twenty-seven minutes in length. Twenty-seven minutes of stillness! A rare occurrence, but a welcome relief as it beat other methods of keeping him calmly in one place, like sitting or lying on him for hours.

Schuyler didn't attend school for two years due to his behavior. Never reported for keeping him out of school, it didn't take much to figure out the district did not want him.

Then the AWOL episodes began. What began as an isolated event soon became a regular occurrence. Sky went missing several times a week. Heading the hunt was Police Officer Kelly…who became a family member. That Schuyler must be watched *every second* could not be taken seriously enough!

In the Beginning

A California girl born in 1952 to parents who'd waited a long time for their only child, I was a happy event after six miscarriages. On the surface, life was all—American middle class, as my mother instilled in me a love of beauty and music, and my father passed on a keen mind, a strong work ethic, and an adventurous spirit.

Both my parents were pilots, which opened the door to the most amazing memories. Working and living were given equal importance.

The business of spiritual growth was left up to my mother, who raised me to be a "good Christian girl." The particular protestant denomination in which I was raised turned out to be one of the most rigid and conservative. No card playing, movies or patent leather shoes. Girls wore dresses and *never* voiced an opinion.

However, progressive California afforded me certain freedoms, such as sleeveless blouses! I attended church three to four times a week until young adulthood.

My parents divorced when I was six. Overnight I became a hindrance instead of a joy, as it appeared I did not please my parents any longer. It was 1958 and divorce was a great source of shame for my mother. Divorced women—especially divorced Christian women—weren't accepted by many in that era.

My father's ability to communicate his love for me was dysfunctional at best. This, coupled with the onslaughts of a desperate ex-wife, strained our time together. We continued to have flying adventures, and he had a talent for helping me think outside the box by showing me how the unobvious could suddenly become obvious. Those adventures still make me smile. His presence in my life ended with his passing in 1999.

Clearly, the joy I once brought my parents so effortlessly dissipated too soon, leaving in its wake the internalized belief that love was not something that came naturally; rather it was something to be earned. From that early age on, I operated under this ugly and sinister dogmatic philosophy—a self-imposed "truth" that permeated everything I did…

My husband and I parted company when Schuyler was twelve—it was too much for us to have a life together and with this child who, as one specialist at UCLA reported after a thirty-day inpatient stay, "…has stumped us…he is as good as he will ever get."

At last count, Schuyler has been hospitalized twenty-three times in his twenty years of life, including three thirty-day stays in psychiatric wards. During one of those stays he almost died from an overdose of mistakenly administered medication.

In all, Schuyler has received thirteen diagnoses. These include a seizure disorder that produces auditory/visual hallucinations displaying similar to schizophrenia, Tourette's syndrome, developmental disability, and obsessive compulsive disorder.

It's like a mismatched patchwork quilt; nothing forms a specific pattern, picture, or story. But through it all, Schuyler's charming personality and pure heart prevail. He sparkles when he smiles!

His bio-chemistry has settled down tremendously, especially now that he's through his hormonal adolescent years. His doctors have finally found a drug cocktail of eight medications that is working well—revisited periodically to avoid long-term damage.

Let Go and Let Godma

Eventually all of my old dogmatic belief systems began to fail me. My natural ability to continue on in spite of Schuyler's challenges became increasingly difficult. After fifteen years, I found myself falling into a deep abyss, with no sight, sound, touch…no hope, no bottom. I had disappeared.

Previously I'd maintained massive pride in my ability to solve problems. After all, I could think outside the box…It was utterly impossible that this innocent child could suffer so! Anger erupted and pervaded all of my thoughts and emotions.

Enraged that first my demands—and then my pleadings—to God, or whoever was "in control," to take *me* if that would bring relief for Schuyler, were met with silence, my previous strength and resolve deserted me completely.

My former "Midas touch" was gone. Friends and family disappeared as well. "Falling" became a normal daily event; and "normal" became hell, right became wrong, hope transformed into illusion, and truths turned to lies. Thus "normal" seemed to promise the only absolute: the slow painful death of me.

After years of defeat, I'd become unrecognizable. Half my hair had fallen out, the remainder turned from naturally curly to straw straight, my gums receded and I developed heart palpitations. Doctors said I was prematurely aging.

As I lay in bed in a fetal position my only thought was: "It's alright my beautiful son. We've only another thirty-five or forty years of this hell. Then we can die and leave this misery. In the *light of eternity* this is but a short trial."

Defeat after defeat had devalued life. What once brought joy now only represented sadness. Nothing had meaning anymore. Finally, I hit the bottom of the abyss. Finally, I stopped falling…it was over. Whatever will be, will be…finally, I LET GO!

But wait…what began as a trickle of thought slowly turned into a stream. The words *"light of eternity"* gripped me. I began to ponder eternity and all things eternal—it became my constant companion of thought. It somehow soothed my soul, my being. Thinking of Schuyler as eternal brought an unbroken connection. No matter what happens he will never stop existing…he will never die.

I was beginning to see everything through the light of eternal connectedness. It was thrilling…similar to when I watched Schuyler discover as a baby all his firsts…he'd embraced each experience with the love and joy of childlike abandonment and, now, so it was for me!

People, animals, nature, even buildings, seemed to illuminate the light of eternity. This energy—this light—is the Divine, the Creator, Source…whatever your name for God. It is you, it is me and it is Schuyler! I now understood; we are all one energy, and nothing is separate.

It was as if the whole universe opened up to me. I realized everything has life…Schuyler has his own agenda for his life and he's working his own universe out and so am I—in the midst of the overall universe we are both the created and the creator; both the drop in the ocean *and* the entire ocean!

Little by little I traded my rigid, dogma-based perspectives for new ones. And I realized that—as energy constantly changes, and constantly creates—it responds to our shifting perspectives. The "truth" of my identity lay in my new-found revelation that I *am* the universe.

My perspective becomes my thoughts, and my thoughts *become* my life experience. Thus, I *create* my life experience. From there, I took the short leap of faith to understand that to ignore the truth of "Godma" is to continue to live under the regime of dogma…

Good news! I am in control…I choose my perspectives! Dogma transformed to Godma! "Godma" unites, promotes freedom, and non-judgmentally encompasses *all* possibilities of experience, not just those promoted by outside doctrine.

What a miraculous discovery! Circumstances, no matter how intense, became less consuming. As fear, anger, and false expectations of myself guided my emotions less and less, they become more and more steady.

I can choose what I think, and I can make my world what it is, but I can stay detached from the outcome. I knew then that I perceived the glass as more than half-full, I perceived it as overflowing!

My truth became glaringly obvious: Schuyler's essence, his spirit, has no special needs. His true self is perfect, whole and complete. I *choose* to see him that way. And in his perfection he is choosing *his* perspectives.

Epilogue

Schuyler, now in his 20's, lives in a group home and is enjoying his life. His light is shining, his chemistry stable, and he is surrounded by the love and support of a wonderfully caring staff and a truly grateful and appreciative mom.

And I shine too; as I spread my passion for helping others find new perspectives and heal their lives, as a certified, licensed trainer and coach of *Heal Your Life*, a program based on the philosophy of Louise Hay.

ABOUT THE AUTHOR: Heather is passionate about sharing the process of creating your world! Prior years of worldly success had turned to a dark chronic and acute care-giving position for her son. Intensity reached beyond previously ample resources....rendering a broken person finding little value to living. Salvation through education changed the tide. Learning we create by our thoughts was key to becoming a Certified/Licensed HEAL YOUR LIFE Teacher/Coach based on the philosophy of Louise Hay....using simple, profound tools in the creation process transforms our thoughts. Transforming thoughts brings new perspectives and creates new life!

Heather Saline
Hope Dynamics
www.HeatherSaline.com
Heather@HeatherSaline.com
805.646.4218

After The Fall
Audrey G. Schoenfeld

I grew up an ordinary kid in an ordinary middle class suburb of Long Island. But my father owned a candy store, and I remember feeling like the richest kid in the neighborhood, able to have all the ice-cream I wanted, pretty much all the time. Coffee was my favorite.

Life seemed normal until I was eleven, when my father fell outside our house as he and my mother were on their way to a movie one night. The details are foggy to me even now, but I do recall the terror that gripped me as I watched him hit the sidewalk.

Weeks later he returned from the hospital in a wheelchair and never left it. He'd been diagnosed with Paget's disease, a chronic disorder that results in enlarged and misshapen bones that, after surgery on his spine, left him permanently disabled. Life was never the same.

I was the youngest of three, two girls and a boy, the boy sandwiched between two very dominant, bossy girls. Not surprisingly, my brother turned out to be a computer nerd, one of those quiet types that can do extraordinary things with a keyboard. He didn't talk much, but fell in love with his high school sweetheart, and spent most of his time escaping to her house after school.

My sister, six years my senior, was practically out of the house when my father became a paraplegic. She escaped right after high school by attending college out of town.

So, there I was, stuck home alone, with my parents. The house was filled with medical contraptions to help make things easier for my father: walker, hand crutches, wheelchair, urinals. But it was clear that nothing was easy for him.

My parents fought a lot, even before this happened, but now they fought even more. When things got really tense, my father would make a grand attempt to get out of the wheelchair and walk. It never worked. Sometimes he cried. My mother cried a lot too, for herself, for him, for us. I cried too, but mainly I bit my nails, and failed at school. Life seemed desolate and fearful.

When I thought things couldn't possibly get worse, they did. A call home from a friend's house one afternoon was greeted by a bunch of hysterical voices at the other end; my mother was in the midst of a grand mal seizure. I remember sitting in the neurologist's cramped office in Manhattan. There we were, trying to understand what this little man behind his big desk was telling us.

My mother had a brain tumor and needed surgery. We had questions, but I don't remember the answers. I do remember assisting my disoriented mother as the doctor asked if I was going to help my father, who was trying to lift himself out of the chair with his walker.

Struck by the enormity of our tragic circumstances, I never felt more alone. My married sister still lived abroad, and my brother had enlisted. It felt like too big a job for such a young person. But there I was, struggling to maintain an air of dignity and decorum as the three of us limped out of his office.

The tumor turned out to be non-cancerous, but left my mother with a bald head, and a number of medications to control seizures. Fine for two years until it grew back, the next surgery rendered her completely paralyzed on the left side of her body. At least she could still function and have some quality of life—until it returned—again, two years later.

By this time I was twenty-three and lived on my own in Manhattan. My parents had home aid assistance and physical therapists, but still much of my life was consumed with worry. On weekends I returned home to care for them.

My mother's third and last surgery left her in a coma and on a respirator, in a state the doctors described as "vegetative." Eyes open, and reflex movements, but no real cognition; she remained that way for two years.

I visited her daily in the facility not far from my apartment. I never really knew how much she could hear or understand. Sometimes she would just stare at me. It scared me. I wondered if she knew me—if she blamed me for being trapped in this condition, this place, this endless black hole.

My siblings, who would be there when they could, and I used to talk about "pulling the plug," but none of us had the nerve to do it.

Then one night in the supermarket across the street from my apartment, as I picked up groceries for dinner, I was suddenly overcome with a huge wave of nausea. I dropped everything and ran, hoping to make it home in time. I heard the phone ringing before I turned the key in the apartment door. It was my father. My mother had just died. I knew immediately my experience in the supermarket was my mother saying goodbye. The nausea passed as I dissolved into a sea of sobs, tinged with an enormous sense of relief. It was over.

Shortly thereafter my father moved into an assisted living home. Reminiscent of his earlier life, he set up a stationery store at the facility. He kept himself busy and seemed happy. Everybody knew and liked him. I hated visiting the place, seeing the old and sick on my way to him or his "store." One of his best friends lived in an iron lung.

My father died exactly five years after my mother. All those hospitals, doctors, medicines—no longer needed now. My parents were gone. I wasn't finished with them, but it seemed they were finished with me. She had been 57, he 65. I felt alone, scared, empty and bereft.

My sister still lived in London, and my brother, although nearby, just wasn't there. Numb, I spent my nights club hopping, partying with friends and strangers, oblivious to the passage of time. Days and nights blurred, and nothing made sense. My life was a mess.

Around this time a friend introduced me to an Ashram on the upper west side. I knew nothing about meditation, had no clue what an "Ashram" was, but it piqued my interest.

The first time I entered the Ashram, the scent of incense, both earthy and herbal, enveloped me. I heard the low hum of chanting coming from an upstairs room. It was a beautiful turn-of-the century townhouse with a commanding exterior, and a warm, mysterious interior, and a sign near the small bench by the door that said "please remove shoes."

Led bare foot to the meditation hall, I entered a huge room containing an altar that held candles, a large photo of the Guru, and a number of men and women sitting cross-legged, separated from each other on either side of the room.

A beautiful young Indian monk lit the incense and offered a prayer. At the end of the ceremony, he bowed down to the Guru's photo. A bell rang, a drum beat, and the evening prayer, or "Arati," began. I then heard one of the most beautiful songs ever, sung entirely in Sanskrit.

Intrigued, I began to spend several evenings a week at the Ashram, singing the prayers and falling in love with the sounds of the Sanskrit syllables on my tongue. We chanted in unison, and meditated quietly. I began to experience a different kind of "connection" with these strangers, one that seemed more spiritual than anything I'd encountered before, even with family and friends.

As I grew more fascinated with this newfound sense of connection and peacefulness, I began to participate in the Ashram's Hatha, or kundalini, yoga practice. A place of peace and rest, I looked forward to the quiet interaction with others who—like me—sought answers to the big questions: What does it mean to be a human being? What is life about? Is there more to it than meets the eye?

Little by little, I began to experience a shift. I started to sense light, after a long, dark, frightening time in the abyss, and that there was something on the other side of all the pain and suffering.

It's believed that by awakening the "shakti," or coiled serpentine kundalini, from the base of the spine to the center of the forehead, every person (or soul) has the ability to reach the level of the Buddha, or Christ or Mohammed.

"Shakti" brings enlightenment and liberation from the ego, and the most direct way of receiving it is by transmittal from the Guru. But this road to enlightenment is not always smooth, and is often accompanied by the tumultuous emotional upsets associated with major life change. It is for this reason that the Guru transmits "shakti" only when the initiate is ready. He alone knows who is ready.

I was excited when I learned the Guru was coming to our Ashram from India, and that I'd be given the opportunity to receive "shakti." During our group meditation, the Guru—an imposing figure at 6' 4," resplendent in his monk's orange robe—wandered through the sea of earnest bodies, transmitting shakti with his touch.

I felt an electric shock soar through my body when he touched me. Simultaneously elated and terrified, I knew I'd never be the same. My arms stretched wide, my heart filled with joy and a sense of awe; I realized this was the beginning of a major transformation—one that opened the door to greater clarity, awareness and a profound sense of "oneness" with all beings.

The guru laughed, and I was filled with gratitude to be invited to this divine and glorious place to meet my true self. Suddenly I realized that the path to the divine takes courage and devotion, and that this path is an ever-evolving one.

As I bowed to the guru *and* to my higher self, I knew my healing had begun. I understood in a flash that everything that happened before had a purpose.

My personal transformation continues through my work as a life coach. As I assist others to identify their challenges and reach a new level of awareness, I help them gain a sense of their true life purpose, just as I attained mine—after the fall.

ABOUT THE AUTHOR: Audrey moved from NYC in 1988 and relocated, with her husband to Columbia County, NY. There, she formed a real estate firm, which is currently operating. In 2004 she felt a strong desire to pursue and complete a degree in psychology. Since then, Audrey has become a certified professional coach fulfilling her desire to help people overcome their obstacles and attain their goals. In addition, Audrey has practiced kundalini yoga and meditation since the mid-seventies and combines coaching and meditation in her practice. She finds this process to be a powerful path to greater health, happiness, success and purpose.

Audrey G. Schoenfeld, CPC
Dynamic Life Choices, LLC
ags@taconic.net
518-392-5992

Perfect Timing and Divine Order

Sue Urda

My knees began to wobble as I walked into the conference room with my business partner. My tongue felt three times bigger than normal and my mouth suddenly became so dry that I could barely speak.

I went to get some water from the water cooler and watched my hand shake as I brought the cup to my lips. Dear God, please get me through this. I wondered if my legs would continue to support me as I was motioned to a chair in the middle of the biggest conference table I'd ever seen.

Fourteen executives from various departments—purchasing, merchandising, sales, and legal—faced us. Fourteen of *them,* and only two of us. Gulp. I realized later that they did all the talking while we sat there trying to listen and breathe. It felt like the longest hour and twenty minutes of my life.

Nearly two months earlier, I'd picked up the phone only to hear my multi-million dollar client report "I don't know if you've heard yet—one of the signs caught fire in the field!" My heart raced. "It wasn't a big deal," she reassured me, "The damage was minimal, and no one was hurt." She sounded calm, so I tried to follow her lead. We'd have to retrieve the sign and do some testing to find out what had happened.

A few weeks later, I received another call, and then another. In all, four of our neon signs had caught fire and we couldn't figure out how or why. One sign was only two weeks old, and the others had been in the field for two years already. That meant they weren't all from a specific batch.

We worked with the client, brought in insurance companies, independent safety investigators, and electrical experts, but all to no avail. No one knew definitively what had occurred. That's when the client called us in to their corporate office for a meeting.

Their solution was that we would be responsible to recall and replace all 22,000 signs in the field. My mind raced to calculate the costs: we'd have to spend more than three and a half million dollars! There was no way.

My business partner Kathy and I left the room in silence and rode the elevator with one of the executives from the meeting. He tried to be pleasant and hopeful. And try though I might to hold them back, a few tears escaped from my burning eyes and slipped down my cheeks.

The hour and a half ride back to the office was pure torture and my mind swirled round and round, as I tried not to panic. Could this business be pulled out from under me too? In this particular moment, I couldn't help but notice I had a hauntingly similar feeling in my gut, as if I somehow knew this was the beginning of the end. How would we make it through?

The similarity to eight years before, when my dad's sudden passing at the tender age of fifty-two led to bankruptcy and the hardship of dealing with difficult legal matters, was striking. At that time I was in business with my dad, and his unexpected passing produced such chaos that I was left with little time to grieve.

Such a dramatic and whirlwind ending to his dream revealed to me the fragility and uncertainty of life, and I realized the importance of making every moment count. His passing turned out to be huge wake-up call for me. I pondered whether it was the reason why—eight years later—my business was falling apart. Perhaps I'd been following his dream and not my own.

Ironically, our company was finally on an upswing. After six years of struggle, orders and money were steadily flowing in. Just the month before, we'd received three design awards, and been named one of the fastest growing private companies in the US. We'd grown to fifty employees, including my brother.

My brother! He'd left a "big time'" job in New York City for what we all thought would be a lifetime partnership opportunity with our company. He'd always wanted to be an entrepreneur and this was his opportunity—but it seemed to be slipping away quickly. What would I say to him?

The next couple months sped by in a blur. After several conversations with our lawyer, and a futile attempt to make a deal with the client for future business in exchange for what they had asked of us, they informed us they could no longer do business with us. The final nail sank into the coffin; no more company.

Powerful Me

For reasons I cannot explain, I felt a sense of peace like none I'd ever experienced before in my adult life. I had no idea what lay ahead, or how I'd earn a living. Recently relocated to a beautiful new home, I carried a fairly large mortgage and had amassed little in terms of savings or investments. I realized I was pretty much on my own, yet I could not deny my feelings of serenity and calm.

Without too much travail, our employees and my brother found positions that suited them. Our bookkeeper even got to take some much needed time off to devote to her mother with Alzheimer's. My guilt, especially about my brother, lessened, as things seemed to be working out okay for everyone.

Soon, in addition to feeling peaceful and calm, I experienced a sense of excitement and child-like glee. I recognized that, for what seemed like the first time in my life, I had no ties. All possibilities were available to me.

Of course, this wasn't true. All things had *always* been available to me, just as they are to everyone else. For me though, this was the first time I really saw it this way, and even more importantly, could really *feel* it. Deep within, I knew my life was about to transform into something truly magical. I had no idea how the magic would manifest, I only I knew that it was destined to be!

My father's words of love and encouragement echoed through my mind: "You can do anything, Susie. You're outstanding!" Since his passing, he'd become a constant, encouraging companion, ever-present in my mind and in my soul.

Around this time, during the process of our business's rapid dissolution, a mind-blowing revelation occurred. My business partner felt it too. We realized that we had *created* the exact situation we were in.

For the past several years, we'd vigilantly focused on our own personal and spiritual development. We studied and practiced with teachers like Anthony Robbins, Wayne Dyer, Marianne Williamson, Brian Tracy, and many others. In this process of self-examination, we set future goals to assist and empower women.

At the time, we weren't sure exactly what direction we'd take, especially since we owned a manufacturing company. The only thing we knew for certain was that we wanted to get out of that business and into something that would better serve the world.

That the power of our vision and desire would manifest in the way that it did still amazes us. To this day, I find it almost unbelievable how everything unfolded so perfectly.

In January 2003, a long-time friend of mine invited me to attend an afternoon tea and workshop for women. I had no idea what to expect; but hey, I'd just lost my business so I was up for anything and decided to attend. What I experienced that day opened an entirely new world to me.

From the moment I walked into the room, I felt excitement, gratitude and connection. The room buzzed with the chatter of women, some who met for the first time, some old friends. The three-hour event included presentations from a charismatic and inspiring woman who'd planned the event, an empowerment coach, and a mother-daughter team who taught us meditation.

Fifty women in all appeared to be seeking the kind of connection offered here. As we engaged in the exercises, discussions and meditation that day, my sense of belonging increased. More than that, I caught a glimpse of my future.

I saw myself in the shoes of the speakers who presented information to us. A voice in my head said "Sue, you can teach what they are teaching. You can share what they are sharing. You can be the connector. You can be a source of motivation and inspiration."

Again I heard my father's voice say "you can do anything!"

I envisioned myself bringing women together, and imagined how I could hold my own events, present workshops to women, and share my heart and soul with them. Overwhelmed with excitement, I suddenly knew this was my future.

I remain forever grateful for being introduced to my path that day. I love what I do on a day-to-day basis. I love the many wonderful women with whom I connect. I love the incredible growth I've experienced professionally, intellectually, and spiritually. And I especially love the way my new path serves me, as well as all the women it touches.

Never could I have planned the specific events that led to this dramatic change in my business life. Nor could I have orchestrated the timing of the meeting that day. And I certainly could never have guessed that the name "Powerful You!," which I thought was going to be the title of my first book, would instead become the name of our women's network.

We chose this name because it not only invites the kinds of feelings we wish to inspire in women, it also sets the tone for strong, collaborative, and spiritual connections. I claimed my power through the adversity of my experiences, and I now gratefully devote my time and energy to helping other women do the same.

I do not fear another loss, despite the fact that I'd lost two businesses to unexpected and uncommon circumstances. I've learned that money, like my businesses, has come and gone over the years, but that it has no real bearing on my true happiness. I am always taken care of when I'm in the moment, doing what I love, and being who I am.

The beautiful synchronicities surrounding the many people, circumstances, and events on my path through life confirm for me that my future will unfold exactly as Spirit intends.

My mantra is "all things happen in perfect timing and divine order," because I know this is *my* truth.

ABOUT THE AUTHOR: Sue Urda, a.k.a. 'The Connections Expert', is an Author, Speaker, Inspirer & Co-Founder of Powerful You! Women's Network. Sue is a two-time honoree on INC Magazine's list of the 500 Fastest-Growing Private Companies. Her award-winning book, *Powerful Intentions Everyday Gratitude: 100 Transformational Days to Create a Life of Joy, Grace and Ease* to help you understand the complex workings of your mind, tap the inner wisdom of your heart & live each day through deliberate creation and intent. Sue assists women in their own pursuit of success, joyful-living & balance. Her mission is to connect women to each other, their visions & themselves.

Sue Urda
Powerful You! Women's Network
www.sueurda.com
info@powerfulyou.com
973-248-1262

The Voice Within

Carol Walkner

No, I'm not crazy. But I do hear voices. And without them, I'd be lost.

The first time I heard the voices coming through loud and clear was in the neighborhood where I grew up in the 1950's—a good section in a large, urban city in New Jersey. At nine years of age, I felt safe as I roller skated, played kick ball with the boys, sold homemade lemonade on the street, and hung out from morning until night.

Then one day three local bullies, between the ages of 11 and 13 decided they wanted to teach me a lesson. I guess they wanted to show me who was in charge of the neighborhood, and they certainly didn't think it was my little 4'5" scrawny stick person self.

Little did they know that what I lacked in height and weight, I made up for in intuition and my ability to run like the wind. So when that inner voice told me to run, I didn't hesitate—I took off in a flash! Listening to the whispers in my head, I dove under a huge bush just as the three bullies rounded the corner.

They passed me right by, never found me, and soon gave up. They never bothered me again. After that, every time I followed the voices of my intuition, my higher self—God, if you will—I have been successful, safe, and happy. By following these voices I've been true to myself, lived my life authentically, with deep passion, and transformed my life many times over.

And when I didn't listen…well…sometimes fate just can't be denied. As I walked down the aisle towards my husband to be (and the future father of my son), the voices cautioned me: "Carol, do you really want to marry this man?"

I don't know! I've had a crush on him since grade school, we've been dating for years and we dance so well together. Isn't that enough? I ignored the voices, continued down the aisle, and said "I do."

The marriage ended after 10 years.

The Voices Don't Lie

A few years later I took the advice of my wise inner voice one night when, not even scheduled to go to work, it virtually screamed at me to go to my workplace. At the time, a single divorced mom living in the Midwest, I not only worked full time *and* part time, but attended school as well.

Unable to ignore my overwhelmingly strong intuition, I finally listened and made my way over to work. Little did I know that my life was about to change in the blink of an eye…once there I found myself in the midst of a surprise audit by an out of town auditing firm. And wouldn't you know it— half of our people hadn't even shown up!

I spent much of the evening beside the accountant to make sure the work was done properly and professionally; I reassured him that all was in order. As we worked, we chatted and I learned that he was divorced, close to my age, and had never traveled outside his home office. He was here only because he and another employee from his firm flipped a coin to see which one would have to make the trip!

We stayed in touch after that night, talking long distance, and within thirteen months we married. Had it not been for my inner voice, I would have missed out on seventeen years with a wonderful man.

There were occasions when that inner voice seemed ridiculous and silly. Like the time I took my son to the store, and the voice in my head kept telling me to take my time getting out of a parking space.

What's the big deal, I thought, how could that one small action mean anything? Within seconds a work van came barreling out of nowhere, slammed into my car and sped off. Had I listened to my wise inner voice and waited those few seconds, the accident would never have happened.

Fortunately neither of us was injured. But the severe damage to my car cost me both money and time. I waited two weeks for the car to return from the shop. Boy did I regret ignoring my intuition...*How stupid;* I thought... *lesson learned, hopefully forever!*

Over the years I purchased cars and houses, attended churches, and made friends—all by listening to that inner voice, that intuition, that God speak. So I knew better than to ignore it when my soul began to dry up and I felt as though I was dying deep inside. The voice and heart of my intuition told me to move on from my 17 year marriage, and I knew it was time to end the relationship.

The Healing Work Begins

Several years ago, I discovered Women Writing For (a) Change, a feminist writing school that teaches specific methods focused on sharing and writing. So profound were the effects of these classes that I signed up for their training program.

Listening to the reading of a contemporary poem at the beginning of each session, each time was like someone turned on a 1,000 watt bulb, shined it on my heart and opened a floodgate of feelings that led to the creation of my own poetry. Since becoming part of this group, I watched so many women in the classes heal from addictions, grief, and illnesses as they wrote from a deep place and shared their work in a safe, sacred space.

I began to pour hundreds of poems onto the page; words that seemed to slither out when I opened up from that heart and soul place deep within. When I re-read some of them now, I don't even recall writing them, but I know they were born of words stuck inside me like splinters.

A while later, back in New Jersey, I found myself once again in the process of reinventing myself. I joined the local chamber of commerce and found myself at one of their networking meetings, sponsored by a local nursing home. The meeting ended, and as people filtered out, the voice in my head told me to approach the nursing home managers.

I listened dutifully and, as I introduced myself told them: "I hold writing circles for senior living, assisted living and nursing home residents to help them write their life stories. They then share their stories with each other and eventually with their families."

I do?

"Wow, you do? That sounds perfect!" responded one manager. "We need an activity just like that for our facilities, and we can give you names of other facilities in the area as well."

I beamed at this woman. "Terrific! I'll give you a call!"

"Great…by the way, what's the name of your business?"

The name of my business? Okay Miss Smarty Voice, get me out of this one!

"The name of my business is Words of Wisdom because our wise elders have so much to say!"

Wow, thank you voice! Way to go—I'm a believer!

The Real Me

My Words of Wisdom writing circles now include not only seniors, but nurses, social workers, those in hospice situations, and women dealing with grief, loss and addiction. The best part is that I use my inner voice as a guide to develop writing prompts that help spark the creative process in others. It's heartwarming to watch participants' lives transform as they express themselves through the written word.

I'll never forget the nurse in her thirties who wrote and shared a story about a tragedy she experienced as a teenager. She never told this story to anyone until the writing circle. There wasn't a dry eye in the group when she was finished. What a cathartic experience for us all! And for her, the result of sharing this tragedy was obvious as she was now able to move on.

In my first senior writing circle, two women who lived in the same facility (in fact, on the same hallway) for seven years discovered that they grew up within blocks of each other! Here they were, 80 year old women, immediately transported back to their individual childhoods with a complete and total understanding of each other as they reminisced about their formative years. I imagined them as eight year olds, holding hands and skipping out the door together, so powerful was their connection now that they had shared something so meaningful.

Motivated by these writing circles, I began to ponder my past. As my mind spanned the years, I remembered when my intuition led me to a well known healer and energy worker through whom I discovered the eastern medical concept of "chi," or the energy that flows though our internal body meridian pathways.

A group of us used ourselves as guinea pigs to develop a system to work with energy to help people stop addictive behaviors. After a few weeks on our new energy program we'd each gained 10 pounds. This was good news for me since I had been battling anorexia for the past twelve years.

It was through this energy work that I realized I had a gift! My life had been like a locked door, but energy work was the key. I was an energy healer!

After that, something clicked inside me and the various facets of my life tumbled into place. Although I would not call myself a medical intuitive, I can *see* energy blockages in the human body. And I can psychically remove them.

Recently, when a business associate mentioned a chronic stomach condition, I asked her if she was made to swallow her words as a child, especially at the dinner table. Her eyes widened. "How did you know?" she asked in disbelief. Before I could even answer she asked me if I'd help her. Since her energy sessions with me her pains have all but disappeared.

How do I tell the ultra-conservative, very conventional people in my life that I *see* the un-seeable, *know* the unknowable? I sensed for so long that many of those closest to me feared my talents…so I swallowed them whole and worked for the past twenty-five years in secret.

But now I trust that my intuition leads me right to those most in need of my gifts *and* my services. To tell my story is to return home. I have found my external voice, and it's like putting on my transformational party shoes to attend the celebration for the voice within…

ABOUT THE AUTHOR: A sales and marketing executive, writer, and teacher for more than 40 years, Carol is a trained and accomplished public speaker, workshop leader and group facilitator. Her business articles appear regularly in trade journals, and her poetry and stories are printed in magazines, journals, and online publications. Certified to teach writing through Women Writing For (a) Change, Carol facilitates therapeutic writing circles for nurses, social workers, caregivers and women. She also works with the elderly to encourage the documentation of personal legacies. Carol holds a B.A. in Journalism from Drake University and an M.A. in Expressive Arts Therapy from St. Mary's University.

Carol Walkner
www.TheDragonWriter.com
513-328-1038

With Gratitude
Acknowledgements

Although our names are on the cover, there are many incredible women who have partnered to birth this inspiring book that you now hold in your hands.

Mostly, it is the 40 authors who have banded in partnership with the desire to share their stories to whom we are grateful. For them, the process has been one of 'digging deep', exposing raw emotions and memories, and countless hours of finding the right words—all with the intention to make an impact on the lives of women who read their stories. These authors are courageous, humble and powerful, and we hold each of them in our hearts.

We have deep appreciation for the experts who have taken part in birthing this book: our editor Sheri Horn-Hasan, our graphic designer Donna LaPlaca. and our business experts—AmondaRose Igoe and Lethia Owens as well as the many other women who have contributed their guidance, expertise, love and support.

Dr. Sue Morter's lessons of truth have been a source of strength that have empowered us to move on our dreams, and step more fully into our path. We are grateful to know her.

We are grateful to our friends and families who enthusiastically and continually support our efforts, projects and crazy ideas—without you our lives would not be so sweet.

Above all, we are grateful to Spirit who constantly tosses gifts before us, provides gentle nudges and insistent pathways. Keep 'em coming!

With much love and gratitude,
Sue Urda and Kathy Fyler

About Sue Urda and Kathy Fyler

Sue and Kathy have been friends for 22 years and business partners since 1994. They have received awards and accolades for their businesses over the years and are currently loving their latest foray into anthology book publishing where they provide a forum for women to achieve their dreams of becoming published authors.

Their pride and joy is Powerful You! Women's Network, which they claim is a gift from Spirit. They love traveling the country producing meetings and tour events to gather women for business, personal and spiritual growth. Their greatest pleasure comes through connecting with the many inspiring and extraordinary women who are a part of their network.

The strength of their partnership lies in their deep respect and understanding of one another as well as their complementary skills and knowledge. Kathy is a self-proclaimed computer geek and technology nut as well as free-thinker. Sue is an author and speaker with a knack for creative undertakings.

Together their energies combine to feed the flames of countless women who are seeking truth, empowerment, joy, peace and connection with themselves, their own spirits and other women.

Reach Sue and Kathy at:
Powerful You! Inc.
3031 Route 9 South #300
Rio Grande, NJ 08242
973-248-1262
info@powerfulyou.com
www.powerfulyou.com

Powerful You! Women's Network
Networking with a Heart

OUR MISSION is to empower women to find their inner wisdom, follow their passion and live rich, authentic lives.

Our Vision

Powerful You! Women's Network is founded upon the belief that women are powerful creators, passionate and compassionate leaders, and the heart and backbone of our world's businesses, homes, and communities.

Our Network welcomes all women from all walks of life. We recognize that diversity in our relationships creates opportunities.

Powerful You! creates and facilitates venues for women who desire to develop connections that will assist in growing their businesses. We aid in the creation of lasting personal relationships and provide insights and tools for women who seek balance, grace and ease in all facets of life.

Our Beliefs

❖ We believe in the power of connections.
❖ We believe in the power of being present.
❖ We believe in the power of relationships.
❖ We believe in the power of women.

We believe in the power of devoted groups of collaborative and grateful individuals coming together for the purpose of personal growth and assisting others in business and in life.

We believe in a Powerful You!

Join or Start a Chapter for Business, Personal & Spiritual Growth
www.powerfulyou.com

Would You Like to Contribute to Our Next Book?

Yes, there will be more!

Do you have a story in you? Most people do.

If you've always wanted to be an author, and you can see yourself partnering with other women to share your story, or if you have found yourself daunted by the prospect of writing a whole book on your own—an anthology book may be your answer.

We are committed to helping women express their voices.

Learn more at:

NEW JERSEY USA

Powerful You! Publishing
3031 Route 9 South #300
Rio Grande, NJ 08242
973-248-1262
powerfulyoupublishing.com